Positioning People in Space

Clip Art for Interior Designers, Architects, Landscape Architects, and Illustrators

MAMDOUH FAYEK

MCGRAW-HILL

NEW YORK   SAN FRANCISCO   WASHINGTON D.C.   AUCKLAND

BOGOTA   CARACAS   LISBON   LONDON   MADRID   MEXICO CITY

MILAN   MONTREAL   NEW DELHI   SAN JUAN   SINGAPORE

SYDNEY   TOKYO   TORONTO

Library of Congress Cataloging-in-Publication Data

Fayek, Mamdouh.
    Positioning people in space : clip art in context for interior designers,
architects, landscape architects, and illustrators / Mamdouh Fayek.
       p.   cm.
    Includes index.
    ISBN 0-07-021949-4
    1. Clip art.   2. Decoration and ornament — Themes, motives.
  I. Title.
NK1530.F35   1997
745.4 — dc21

                                            97-28554
                                              CIP

*To my mother Ihsan
and my wife Nabila*

TABLE OF CONTENTS

ACKNOWLEDGEMENTS

This book materialized as a result of the urging need expressed by my wonderful students over the years. Their great confidence in my capability of developing such a book was a driving force throughout this publication.

Hundreds of thanks are in order for all the anonymous photographers across the globe whose work formed the basis for most of the images in this book. It would have been unimaginable to sketch 1500 drawings using live models.

Thanks are due to Wendy Lochner, the senior editor of the Architecture and Design Division at McGraw Hill, who recognized the freshness and usefullness of my concept and provided me with the opportunity to share it with the world. Her encouragement to produce this publication was much appreciated.

Special thanks go to my twin proteges Gary and Robert Williams, as well as their dad Gary Sr. for scanning all my drawings. The twins executed all my page layouts, chapter seperators, and the book cover, enduring my endless revisions.

Last but not least, thanks to my wife Nabila for her encouragement and belief in me. During the production of this book, and as always, she demonstrated infinite patience while I was absorbed in my work.

INTRODUCTION

For over twenty years, I have been teaching and helping my students place drawings of people in their perspective illustrations. Recently, I have included examples of people placement in design illustrations to assist the students in my classes. Since these examples became quickly overused, it was apparent that a new reference work was needed, and I took on the challenge.

The gamut of space design is constantly widening, and *entourage* drawing styles must vary to suit different design needs and directions. Postures and attitudes should be projected to complement the design presentation. Based on this premise, the book is segmented into topics that give penetrating insight into the suitability of people in the design of useful space.

Interior and exterior perspective drawings are often instrumental in successfully presenting project proposals in a persuasive manner. However, it is often not enough to present only orthographic and parallel projection. Indicating people in perspective views adds instant life, proportion, and credibility to the presentation, and ensures effective design communication. Presentations for commercial versus residential spaces require different approaches and the use of *entourage* provides credibility and proportion to an illustration.

Further, to make an interior perspective credible, several elements must be well presented. The key element is how the space is intended to be used. This should be demonstrated as anthropometrically proportionate and comfortable within a space. The user of the space needs to blend with the view and not be a distraction. As an example, a silhouette or partial contour line that leads the viewer's eyes into the described space may be used to emphasize the depth of the space.

Since the indication of people in perspective concept illustration must also reflect the times, and even project into the future, the whole outlook and posture of *entourage* should include hairstyles, clothes, and posture to amplify the illustration's effect. Most of the drawings presented in this book are deliberately detailed to serve as examples of these techniques and may be used as the basis for interpretation and/or simplification.

The book covers *entourage* that can be indicated in the following areas of space design:

> Exterior Design, which covers different categories and species of vegetation from large trees to hedges. It also includes different types of moving vehicles, from antique to futuristic.

> Retail Design includes shops, boutiques, and department stores showing different groups of shoppers, sales people at work, and display mannequins.

> Office Design includes different working environments ranging from CEO offices, to group meetings, to impromptu meetings, to workers in different operating modes.

> Healthcare Design covers different working situations involving doctors, nurses, patients, hospital and surgery rooms. It also includes different settings regarding ADA (Ameicans with Disabilities Act).

> Hospitality design addresses different setups varying from coffee shops, to cafes, to bars, to restaurants, to hotel lobbies, and hotel rooms.

> Residential Design encompasses different parts of residences: from kitchens to dining rooms, to living/media rooms, to bedrooms, to bathrooms and patios.

This book also includes a category that is not addressed in similar publications, which is accessories. This publication covers accessories in subcategories of indoor plants, bonsai, floral arrangments, and objets d'art. This latter subcategory covers many ethnic and historical indications from primitive to modern abstract.

Chapters one through seven include a host of categorized *entourage* in different modes and postures. Thr reader can hopefully find in these chapters any *entourage* indication not covered under the mentioned topics above. Chapter four covers *entourage* for different groups and cultural representations. *Entourage* for museums, galleries, and antique shops are represented in chapter five. People of different walks of life are indicated in this chapter, in elevational orthographic posture and scale. They can be conveniently used in elevational style presentations. The first chapter is somewhat instructional. It reintroduces the reader to basic human anatomy and measurements. It then presents a myriad of examples of simplified figures. A host of figures in different styles and techniques are also presented. The chapter also teaches how to correctly indicate *entourage* within perspective systems with appropriate cast shadow.

Although many of the figures and drawings shown were derived from thousands of researched and interpreted photographs, extracted from several national and international publications, other figures are purely the creation of the author. Any of these drawings may be scanned into your computer, and be manipulated to suit specific situations.

I hope this book helps students and design professionals alike to increase their knowledge, skill, and use of *entourage*.

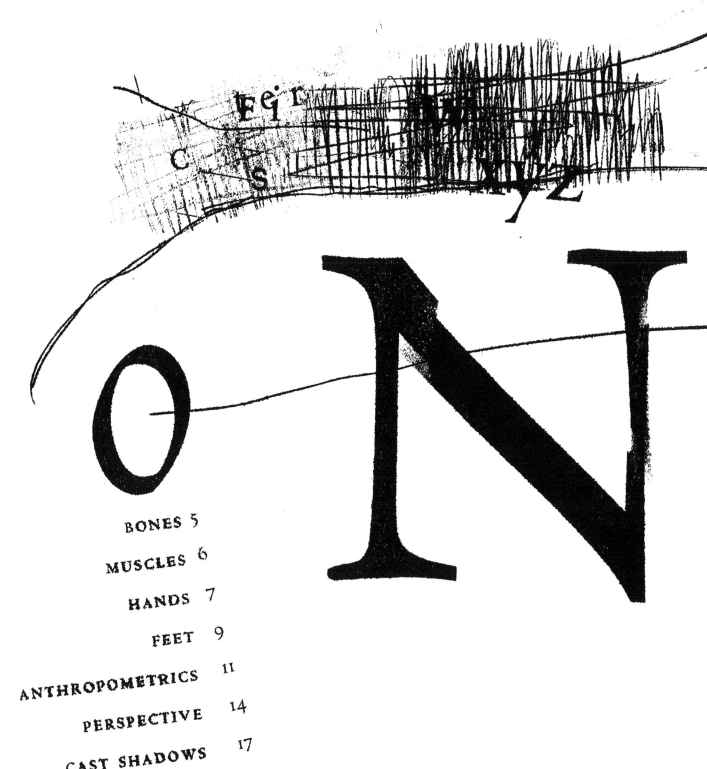

MUSCLES 6

HANDS 7

FEET 9

ANTHROPOMETRICS 11

PERSPECTIVE 14

CAST SHADOWS 17

SIMPLIFICATION 24

STYLES 35

BEFORE AND AFTER 45

cHapter onE

E

INFORMATION

1

INFORMATION

The main purpose of this chapter is to help the reader use this book. The chapter begins with introducing the basic structure of the human body, mainly bones and muscles. I have observed over the years that most people have difficulty indicating hands and feet. I believe it would help to have a better understanding of how these parts of the body are constructed and how they can be indicated. Special attention has been given to drawing hands and feet throughout the book.

Anthropometric measurements are also introduced to give readers more specific information. Throughout the book, there is an emphasis on style. In this chapter, a variety of styles are introduced in a subchapter dedicated to this topic. It provides the flexibility to select the style most suited to the project presentation at hand.

Simplification is presented in another subchapter. It assists the reader in reducing detailed drawings to smaller simplified versions. The examples depicted in this subchapter are echoed later in other chapters.

This chapter also presents examples of views before and after using *entourage*. In addition, it addresses and helps alleviate potential problems of perspective drawing and cast shadow.

Anatomy-Bones

The human body's framework is made of the skeletal bones. There are approximately 206 bones in the human body. Countless movements are facilitated by the way these bones are fitted together and joined by muscles. The spine is most flexible because it contains many small bones. Similarly, the hand is capable of numerous movements due to the many bones it comprises.

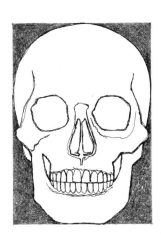

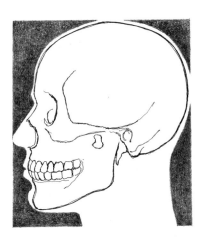

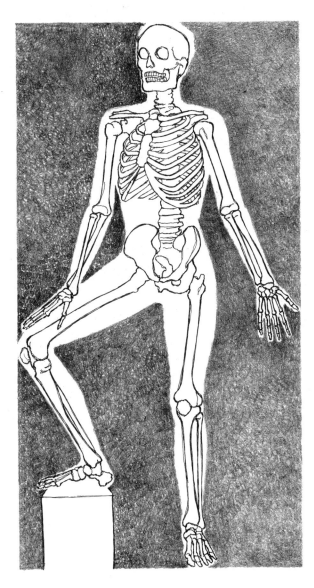

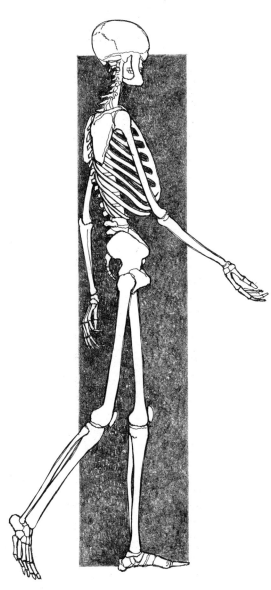

Anatomy-Muscles

Muscles give the body its final exterior form. The number of muscles in the human body is far more than the number of bones. Reasonable visual understanding of these drawings and how the muscles shape the body can help elevate skills of indicating people to higher levels. This is particularly important when positioning people in lively and animated postures.

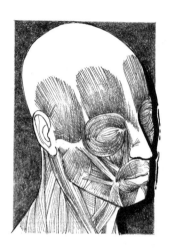

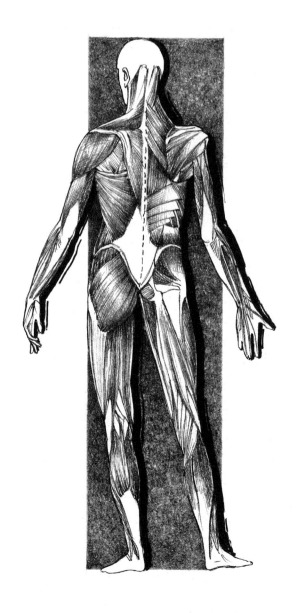

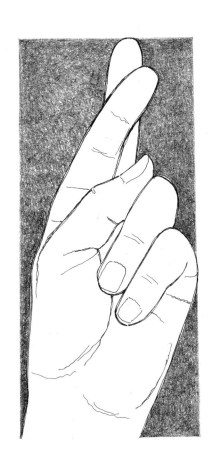

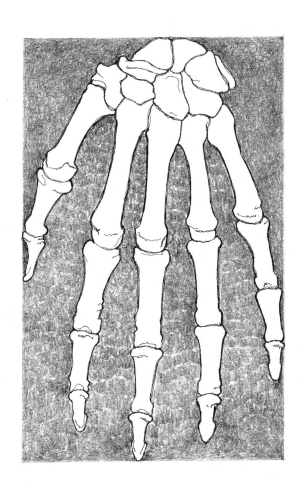

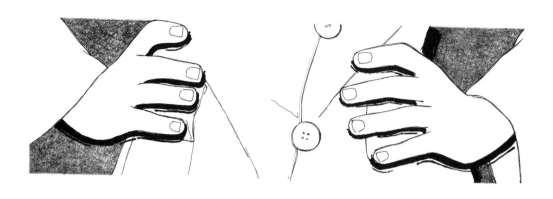

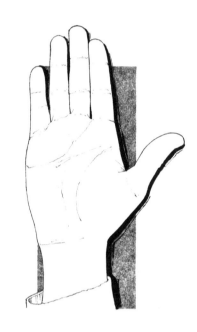

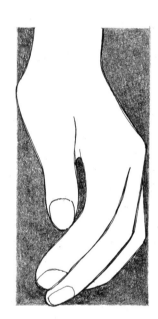

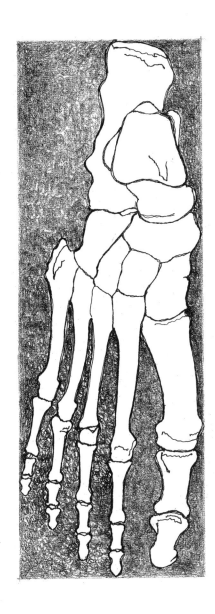
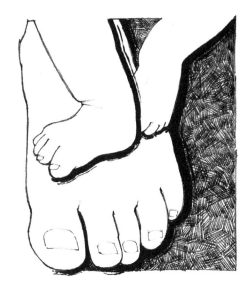
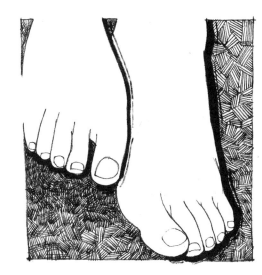
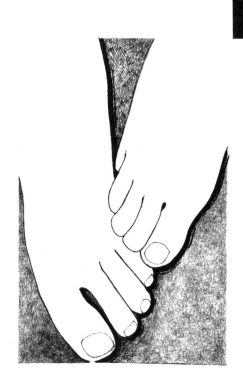

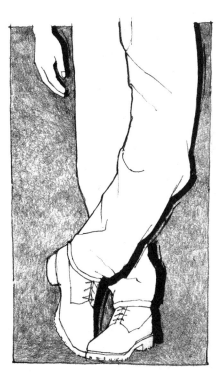

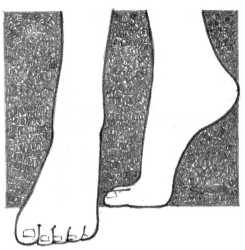

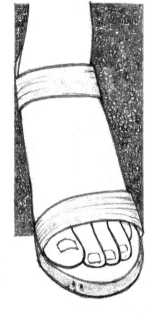

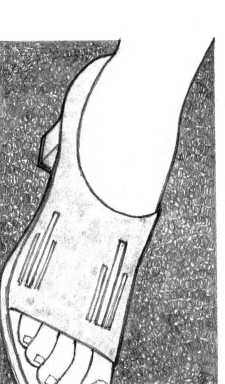

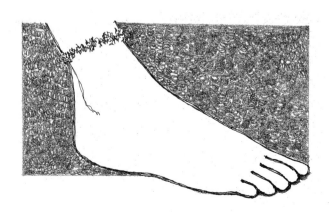

Anthropometrics

One of the main purposes of this *entourage* book is to provide as much pedagogical information as possible to raise the reader/user's level of familiarity with the subject above a mere tracing file level.

Several sources were used to determine the dimensions mentioned in this subchapter. Those users who need more detailed anthropometric information can refer to *Human Dimensions and Interior Space* by Julius Panero or to *Architectural Graphic Standards* by Harold Sleeper et al.

In order to simplify the use of this subchapter, 50 percentile measurements in inches and centimeters were indicated for an age range of 25-34 years. Weight for the average male is 162 lbs. (73.5 kg), and for the average female 131 lbs. (54.4 kg).

People in higher percentiles are bigger and taller, whereas people in lower percentile are smaller and shorter. As people advance in age, their dimensions get slightly smaller.

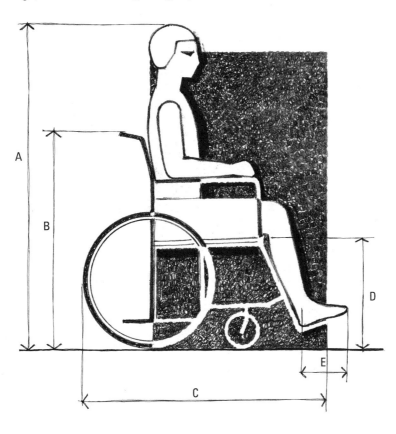

MEASUREMENT	SYMBOL USED	GENDER	DIMENSION (INCHES)	DIMENSION (CM)
Head Height	A	Male	51.50	130.8
		Female	47.00	119.4
Back Height	B	Male/Female	36.00	91.4
Side elevation	C	Male/Female	42.00	106.7
Seat height	D	Male/Female	19.00	48.3
Foot extension	E	Male	8.75	22.2
		Female	7.00	17.8

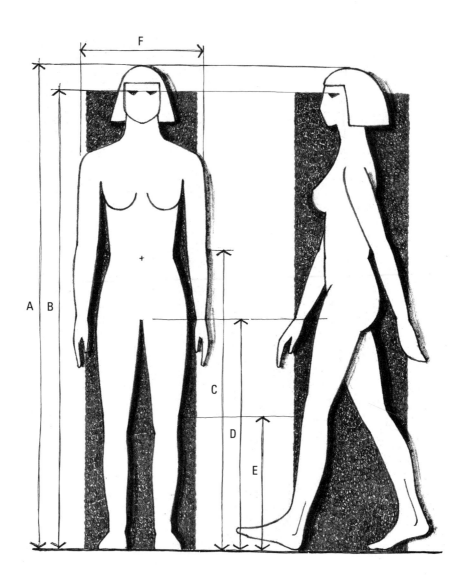

Female Measurements

MEASUREMENT	SYMBOL USED	DIMENSION (INCHES)	DIMENSION (CM)
Stature	A	62.80	159.50
Eye height	B	60.20	152.90
Elbow height	C	41.10	104.14
Crotch height	D	29.40	74.60
Knee height	E	19.40	49.30
Shoulder breadth	F	16.80	42.67

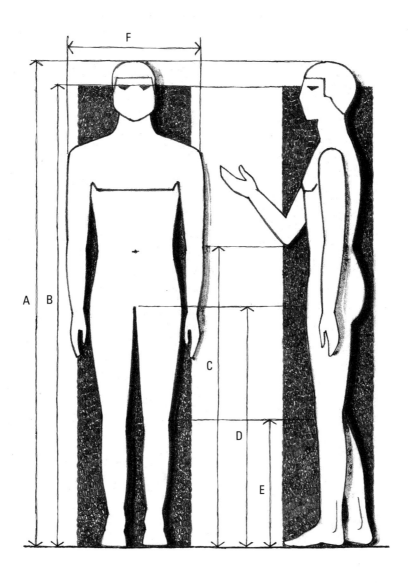

Male Measurements

MEASUREMENT	SYMBOL USED	DIMENSION (INCHES)	DIMENSION (CM)
Stature	A	68.10	173.00
Eye height	B	64.70	164.30
Elbow height	C	44.30	112.52
Crotch height	D	33.50	85.10
Knee height	E	21.20	53.80
Shoulder breadth	F	19.15	48.64

Perspective

While a perspective drawing basically follows the rules of geometry in its construction methods it has to reflect the designer's vision of a space or a view. Envisioning a space design, for study or presentation, needs supporting elements to demonstrate its concept. Such elements consists of the contents (furniture, cabinetry, light fixtures, etc.), as well as representation of the user (human figures). Positioning *entourage* proportionally adds instant credibility to the concept, even in very early design stages.

The user/reader is encouraged to pay special attention to the shoulder direction, as well as the foot placement. To avoid stiffness, positioning may require extra vanishing points on the horizon line as *entourage* indications are rotated off the original grid pattern.

One-point/multi-point system

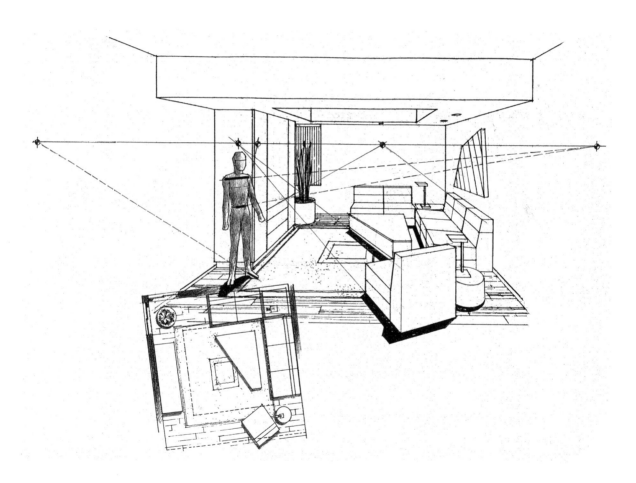

Two-Point/multi-point system

A two point/multi-point system of perspective was used in this drawing. Awareness of the space plan made it possible to use this system. This drawing was specifically selected to familiarize the reader/user, students in particular, with different space design situations.

Three different styles of *entourage* indications are used in the drawing to give the user/reader freedom of choice. However, I do not advise using more than one style in the same drawing. I recommend, especially to the students, to use the *entourage* most suited to the design style being presented. This provides an opportunity to develop personal preferences.

Tapered-one-point system

In my opinion, the most allusive and interesting perspective system is the tapered-one-point. However, most students have difficulty using this system. It requires personal eye-balling judgement regarding the tapering angle and the foreshortening quality of the drawing. Therefore, it is inadvisable for perspective instructors to teach this system to beginner students.

The 1x1 foot floor grid is the major tool used to check the scale for proper positioning in relation to the vertical measurements and the horizon line.

In this drawing, a tapered picture plane was established with a 10 foot high ceiling and a 6 foot horizon line. A 6x6 foot module was created using scaled 1 foot increments of the vertical measuring line starting from the right corner. *Entourage* examples were then selected from different chapters, and positioned using the grid, the picture plane, and the horizon line. Selected drawings were reduced to the appropriate scale to create a live space.

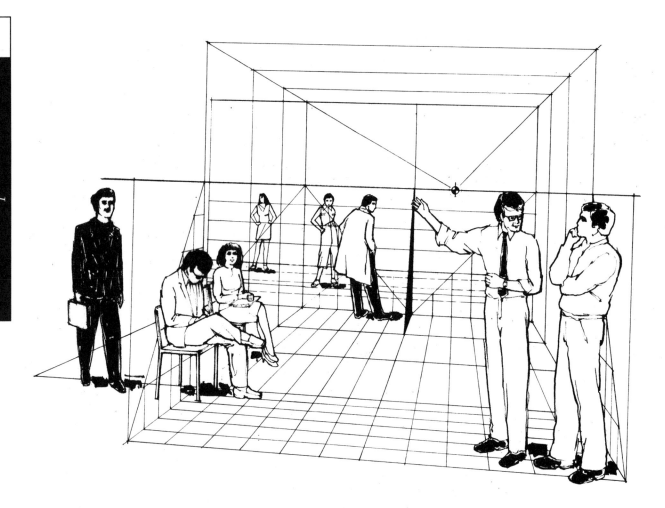

Cast Shadow

Light makes all objects and forms visible. When sunlight or artificial light encounters in its path any physical form, it causes a cast shadow of the obstructing object to appear on adjacent surfaces. The most common surface on which the cast shadow is seen is the horizontal ground plane. If the shadow encounters another form or a particular terrain in its path, it conforms to its shape. The nature of the terrain or object on which cast shadow appears is a determining factor for the resulting shadow. Generally, the shadow bearing direction vanishing point always lies on the horizon line which represents the flat ground.

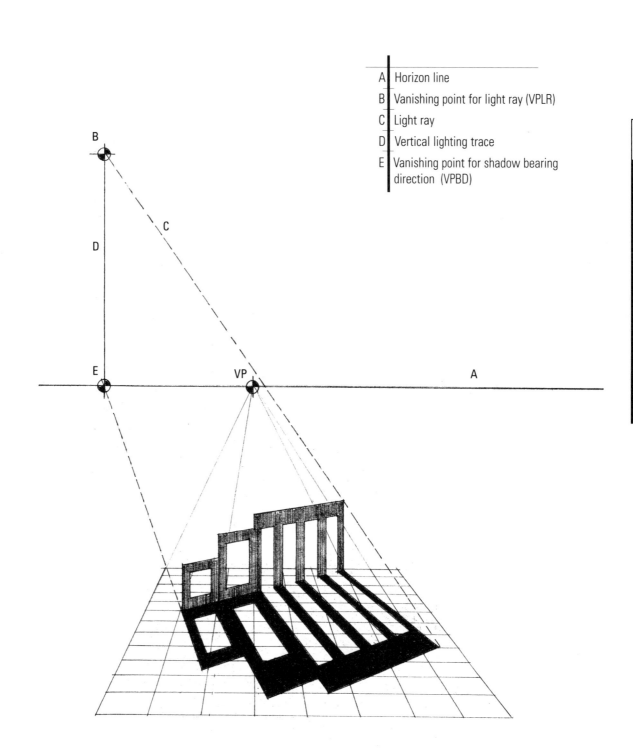

A	Horizon line
B	Vanishing point for light ray (VPLR)
C	Light ray
D	Vertical lighting trace
E	Vanishing point for shadow bearing direction (VPBD)

There are two basic methods for casting shadows:

The Convergent Method:

In this system there are two vanishing points: one for the light source, and the other for the bearing direction of the shadow. The two points are tied by a vertical trace connecting the light source (VPLR) with the bearing direction vanishing point (VPBD), which is always on the horizon line (HL).

If the light source is facing the viewer (positive light) it will cast shadow of the form or object towards the viewer. This is indicated by the position of the (VPLR) above the horizon line. If the light source is behind the viewer (negative light), it will cast shadow of the form or object away from the viewer. This is indicated by the position of the (VPBD) below the horizon line.

A Horizon line

B Vanishing point for light ray (VPLR)

C Light ray

D Vertical lighting trace

E Vanishing point for shadow bearing direction (VPBD)

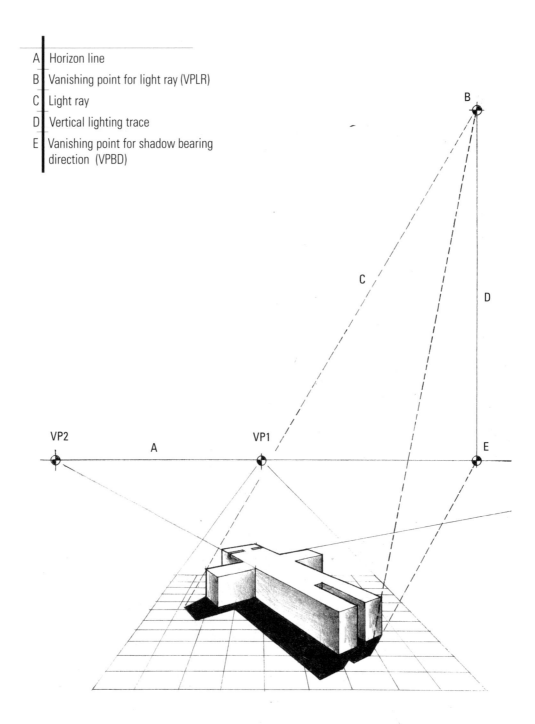

The Parallel Method:

This system is a simplified and convenient interpretation of the vanishing system. No vanishing points are used in this method. It is assumed that both the light rays and shadow lines are parallel in one drawing.

To follow this method, an adjustable triangle is a necessary tool. One angle is selected for the light, and another for the shadow based on the specific problem at hand. These angles are locked throughout the drawing. In interior spaces it is best to use acute light angles, to minimize the amount of shadow. This prevents the overwhelming presence of shadow and provides the necessary form definition. It also eliminates the feeling of floating furniture and objects.

B Light ray
C Shadow bearing direction

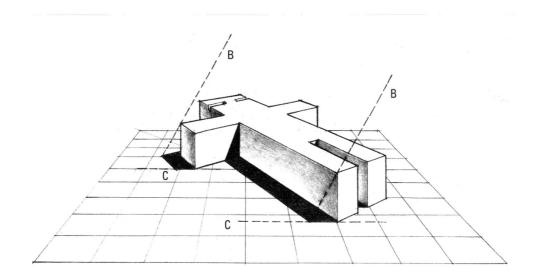

Parallel Positive Light

For an example of the parallel shadow system, I used my interpretation of a bronze portrait by Kurt Schwippert. In this example, light originates from behind the portrait (positive light). On the resulting core, a number of points were selected from which construction lines are vertically brought down to a horizontal drip line. Parallel light rays intersect with those points at the ground plane, where they meet and form parallel shadow bearing direction lines.

A | Light rays
B | Shadow bearing direction
C | Core
D | Drip line

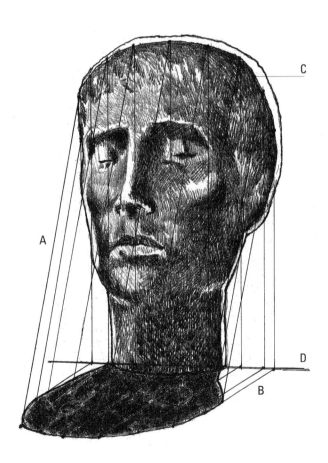

Parallel Negative Light

In another example of the parallel shadow system, I used my interpretation af an Isamu Noguchi Greek marble statue. The sculpture is of a geometric/biomorphic character sitting on a base. The same concept of core and drip line was implemented.

A	Light rays
B	Shadow bearing direction
C	Core
D	Drip line

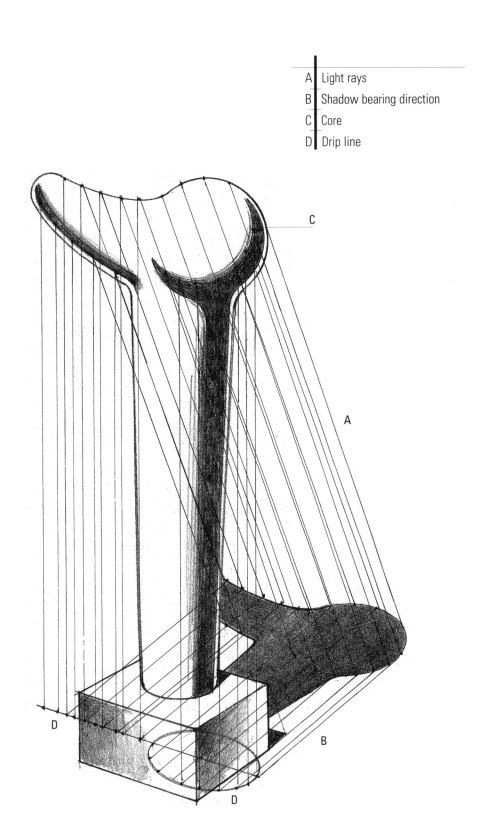

Preferred Cast Shadow

These three examples demonstrate a suitable amount and direction of cast shadow for *entourage*. For better design communication it is advisable to use the preferred example.

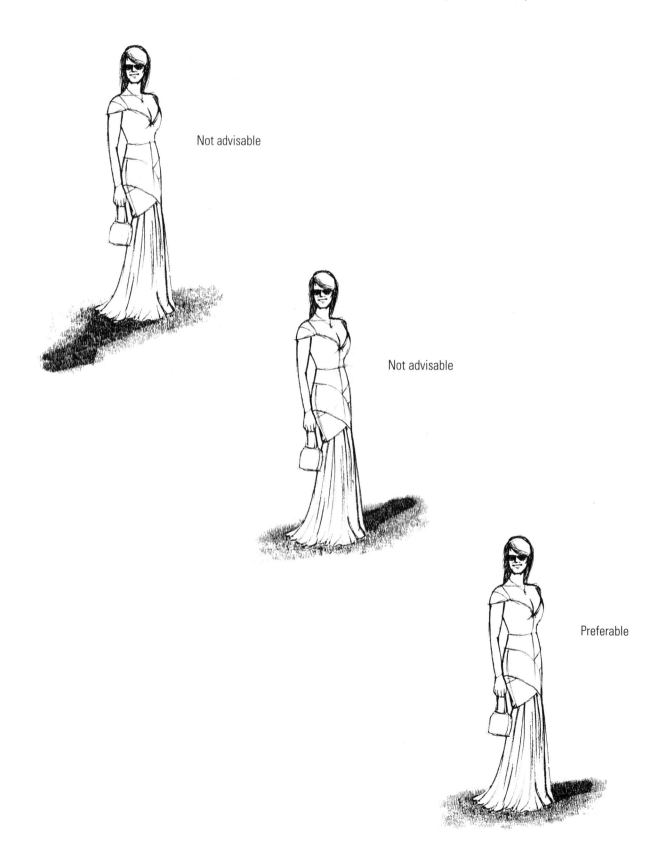

Not advisable

Not advisable

Preferable

Compatible Cast Shadow Style

These examples show the compatibility of gesture cast shadow with loose style as opposed to sharp lined *entourage*. Defined cast shadow is more suitable for sharp lined *entourage*.

Compatible

Compatible

Incompatible

Preferable

Simplification

There are three fundamental criteria for human figure simplification:

1. Reducing the drawing to the basic axial nature of the figure/posture.
2. Reducing the figure to its basic geometric components.
3. Reducing the level of details from the drawing as it is placed deeper in the diminishing perspective view.

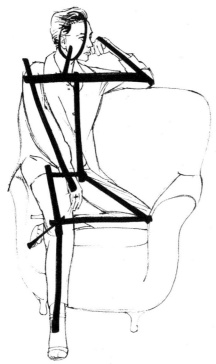

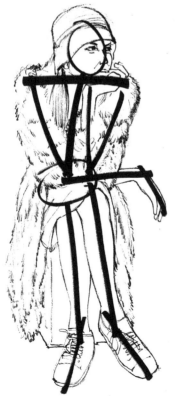

Styles

Based on the direction and style of the design at hand and on the presentation intent, the reader/user should be able to:

1. Select any of the exemplified styles presented in this subchapter.
2. Create a style to use by adapting any suitable drawing presented in this book.

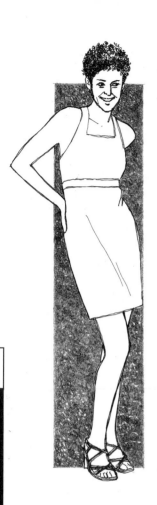

Styles

Before and After views

The purpose of this section is to give examples of *entourage* to emphasize the importance of its use in perspective presentations.

The *entourage* in these drawings was taken from different chapters in the book as applicable to the situation. This was done to demonstrate the selection process and suitability of specific figures and postures to an interior space.

The most important criteria to which all drawings included in this book were selected are:

1. Clarity of form and posture that can be traced, reinterpreted, modified or simplified by the reader/user.
2. Avoidance of overused postures.
3. Degree of usefullness of each drawing to the reader/user, targeting a wide variety of space specializations.
4. Stimulation of the reader/user's own imagination in interpreting the drawings to create persuasive presentations.

It is to be noted that emphasizing perspective depth often requires selecting more than one human figure within a drawing. The reader/user is encouraged to adapt the simplified drawings included in the book for use in more complex situations. Simplification steps and examples are also available for the reader/user to follow.

Before and After examples:
- A retail store
- A residential kitchen
- A hospital room

Before

Before

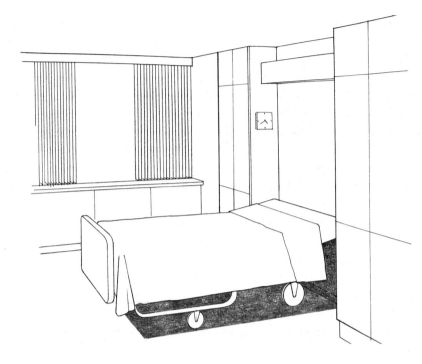

Before

chapter two

people I

2

PEOPLE I

This chapter deals with the biological and behavioral growth of humans. It was intended to be as comprehensive as possible by breaking down the subchapters into some detail without redundancy. While there may not be a need for newly born representation, expecting mothers are represented.

Toddlers were portrayed before kids. Innocence and charm needed to be emphasized in the selected drawings. Preteenage period was represented as a very legitimate stage of complex growth to precede the volatile stage of teenage. This was followed by a wider section of youth. Choices were made to portray a comprehensive cross-section of individuals during this attractive and energetic age.

It didn't seem appropriate that only slim and trim people should be portrayed. People with larger sizes needed to be represented as well.

As our population is aging, senior representation had to be included in insightful situations and postures to induce positive reactions from the reader/user. Projects of retirement homes and co-housing as well as many similar projects can be helped by this reference.

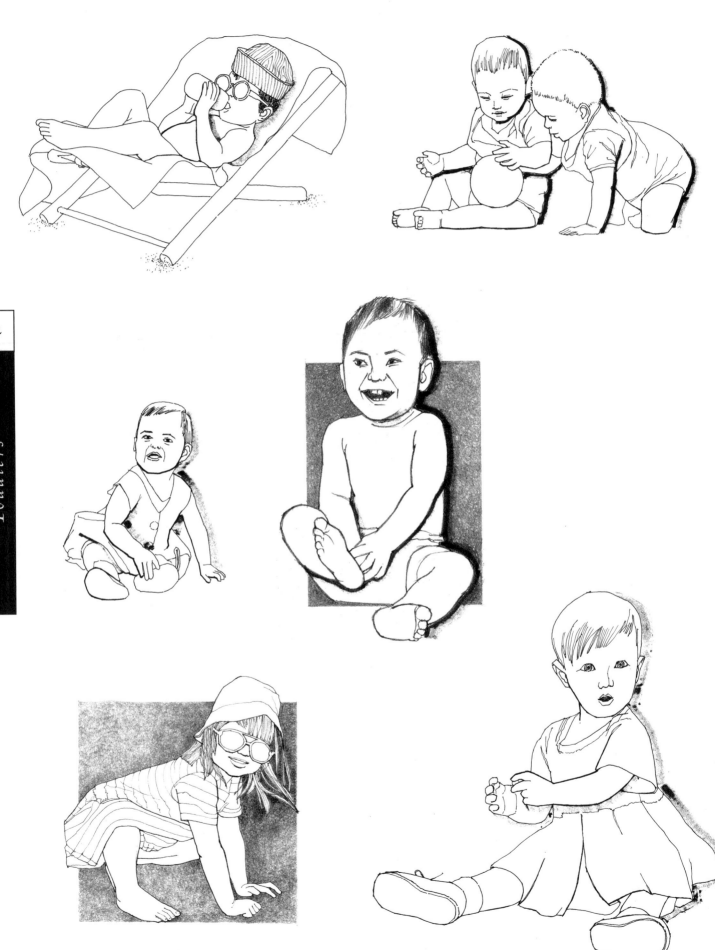

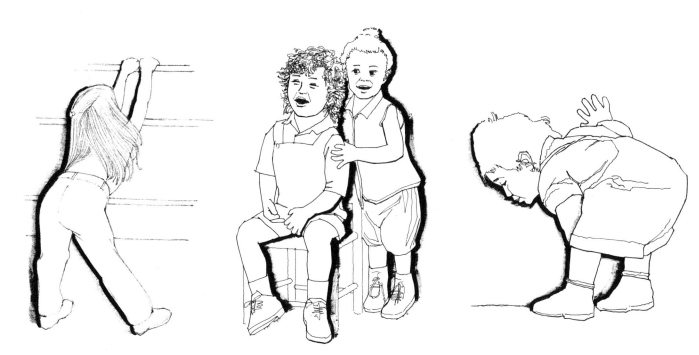

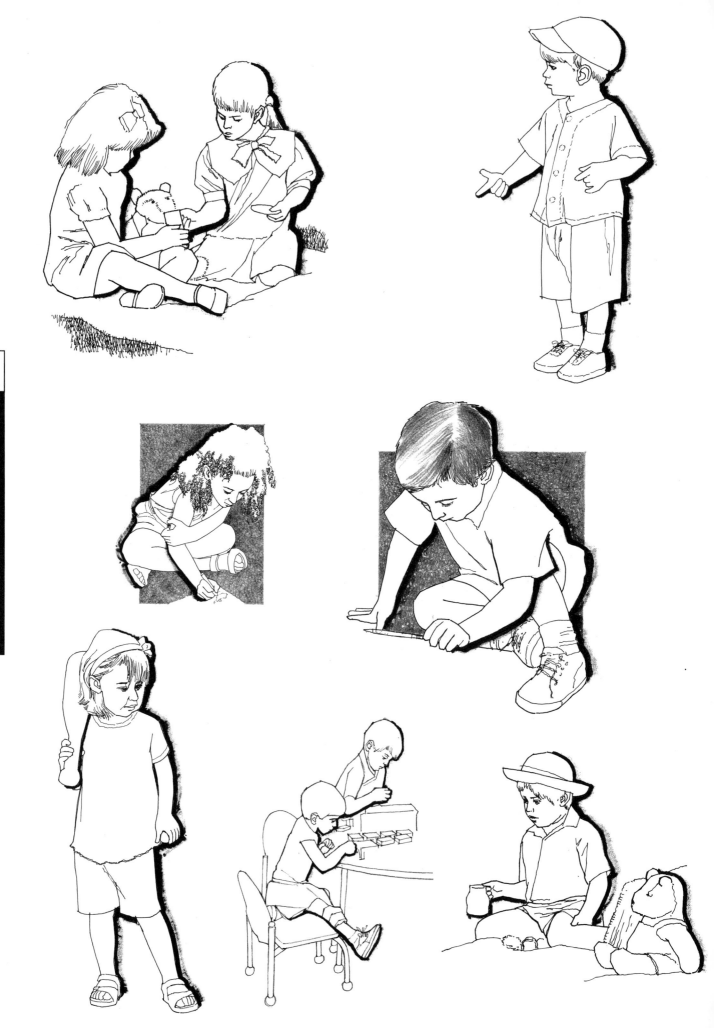

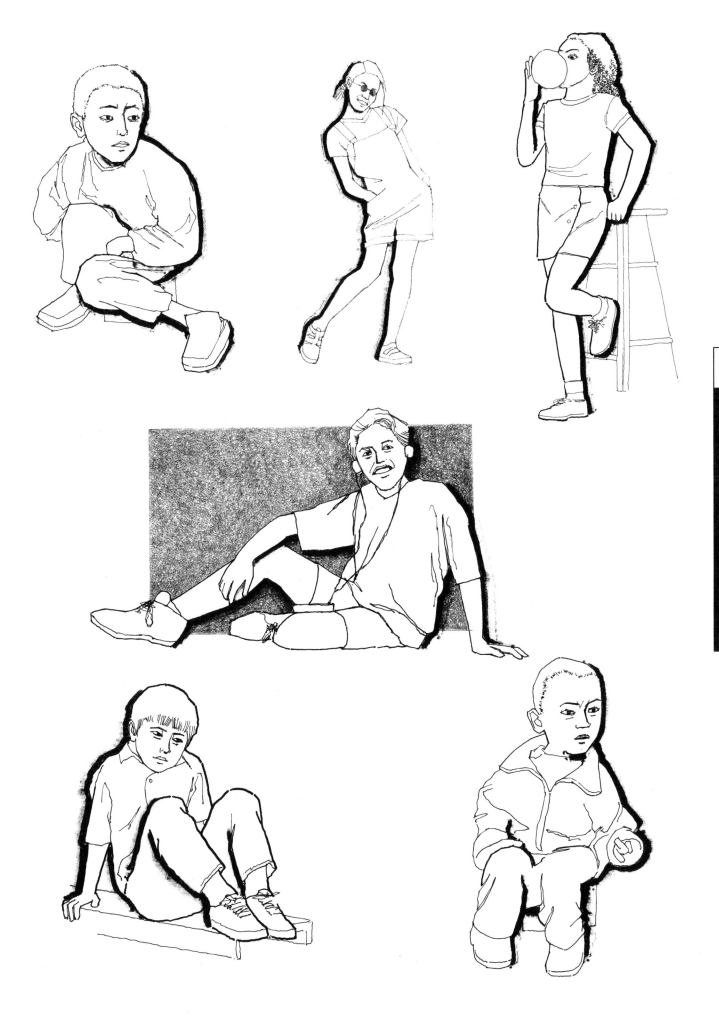

Preteens

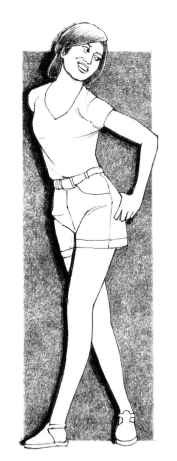

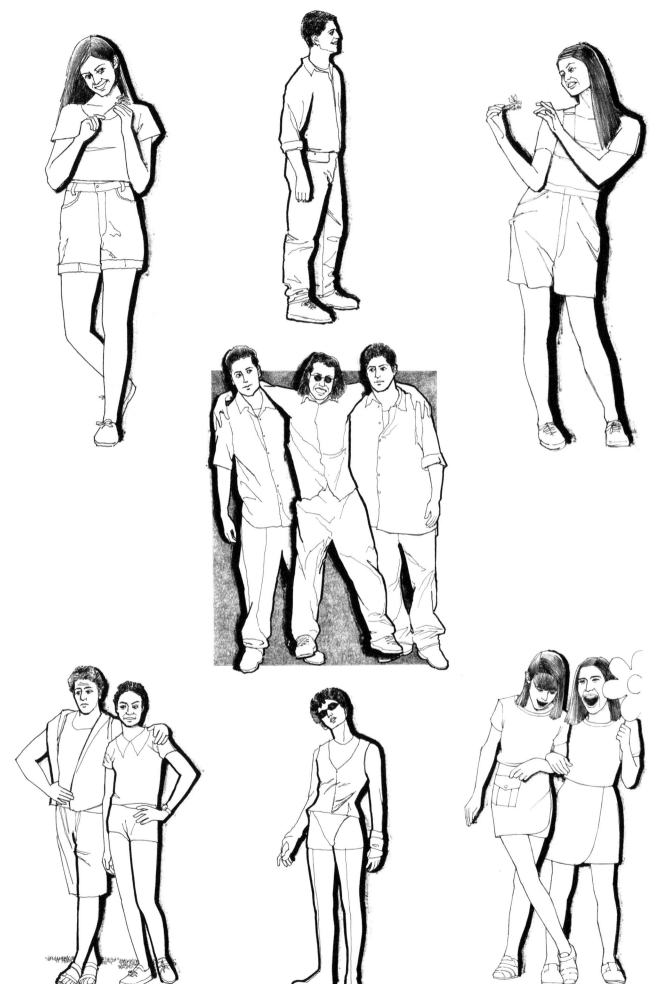

Youths

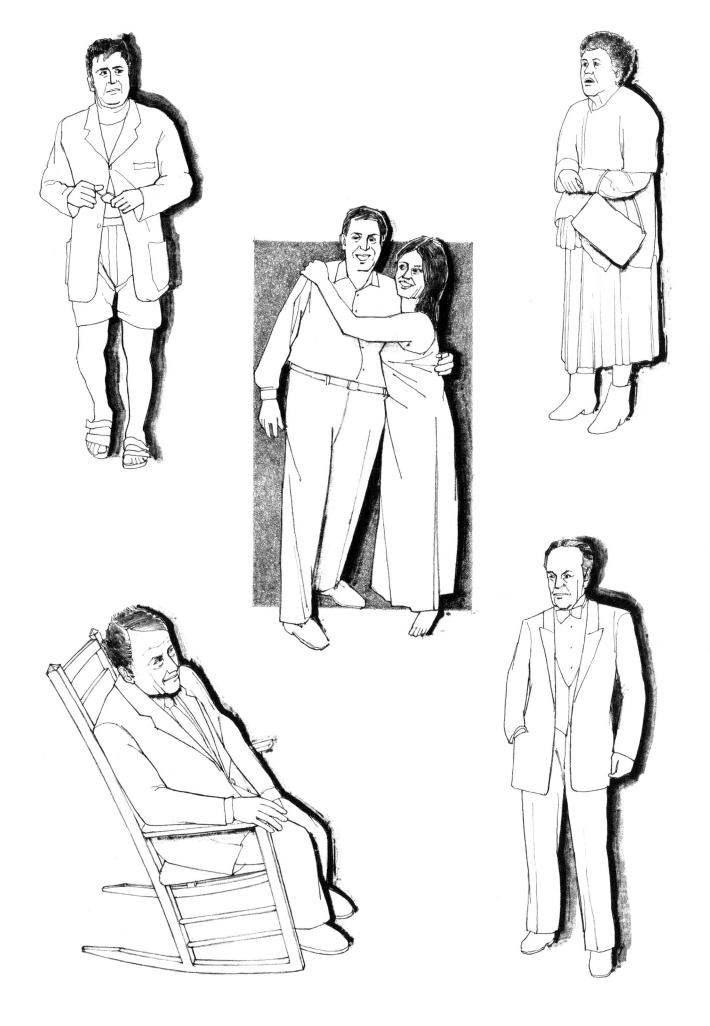

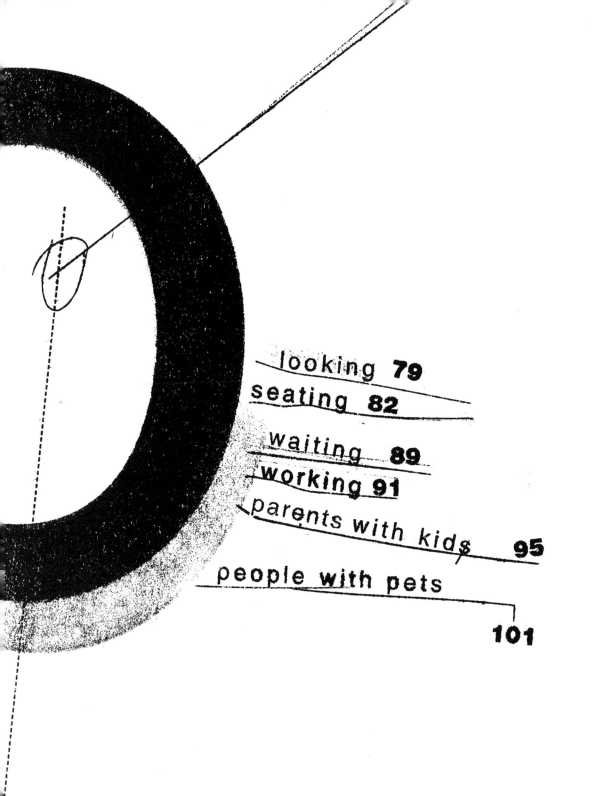

[CHAPTER THREE]

people II

PEOPLE II

Effort in this chapter was exerted to widen the range of selection for the reader/user based on the spirit and style of the project presentation at hand.

People in natural, everyday situations were indicated. Insightful choices were made to allow the users to engage their own imagination in the selection of the postures and eventually the style of indication in their specific projects by relating to the first chapter.

The purpose of this approach is to assist in giving or adding life to project presentations which can induce client and viewer enthusiasm and approval.

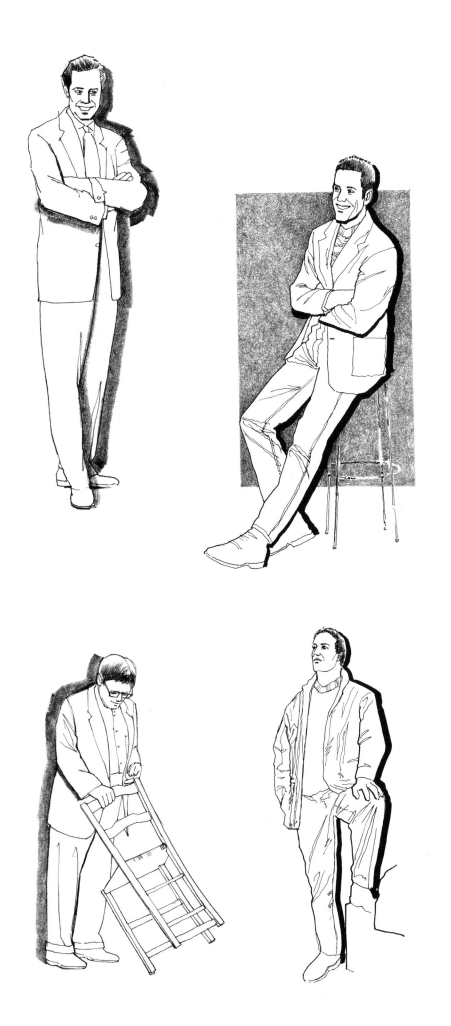

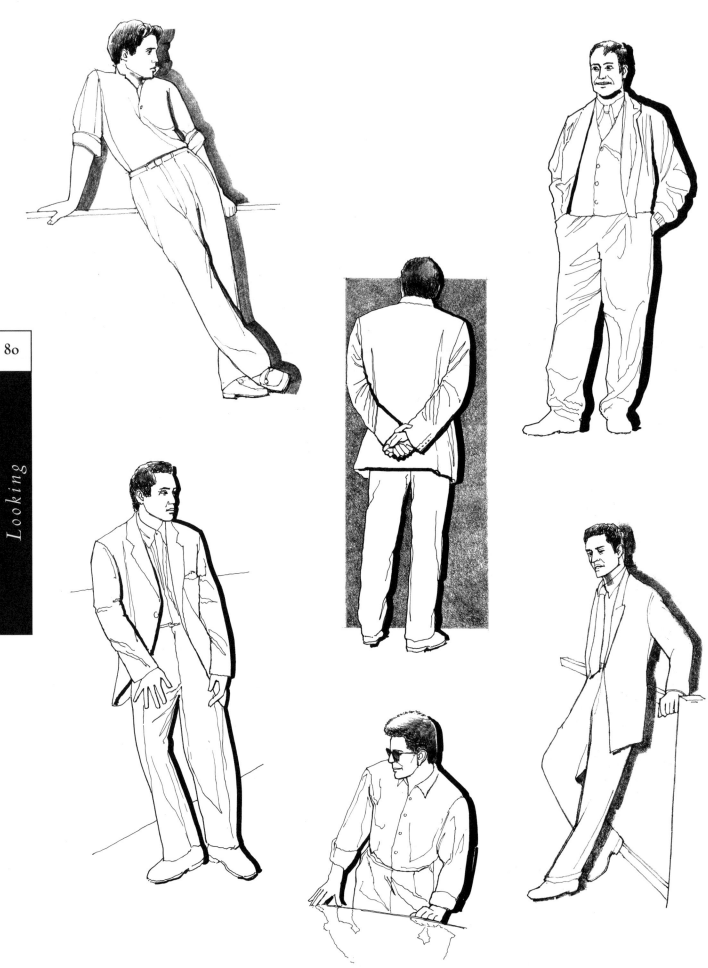

Seating

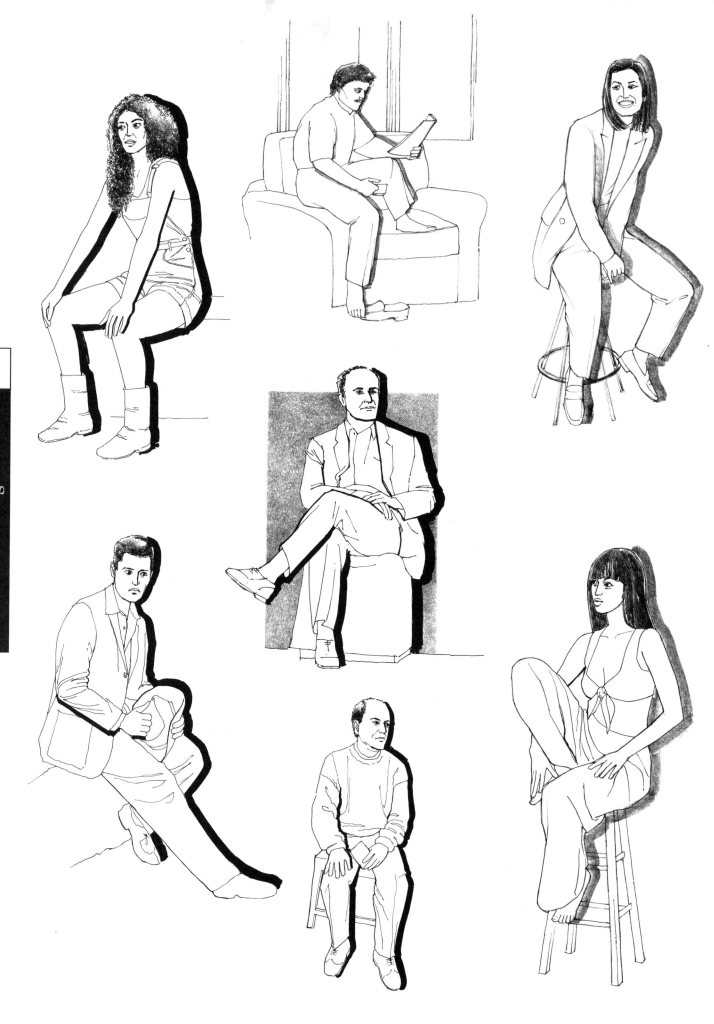

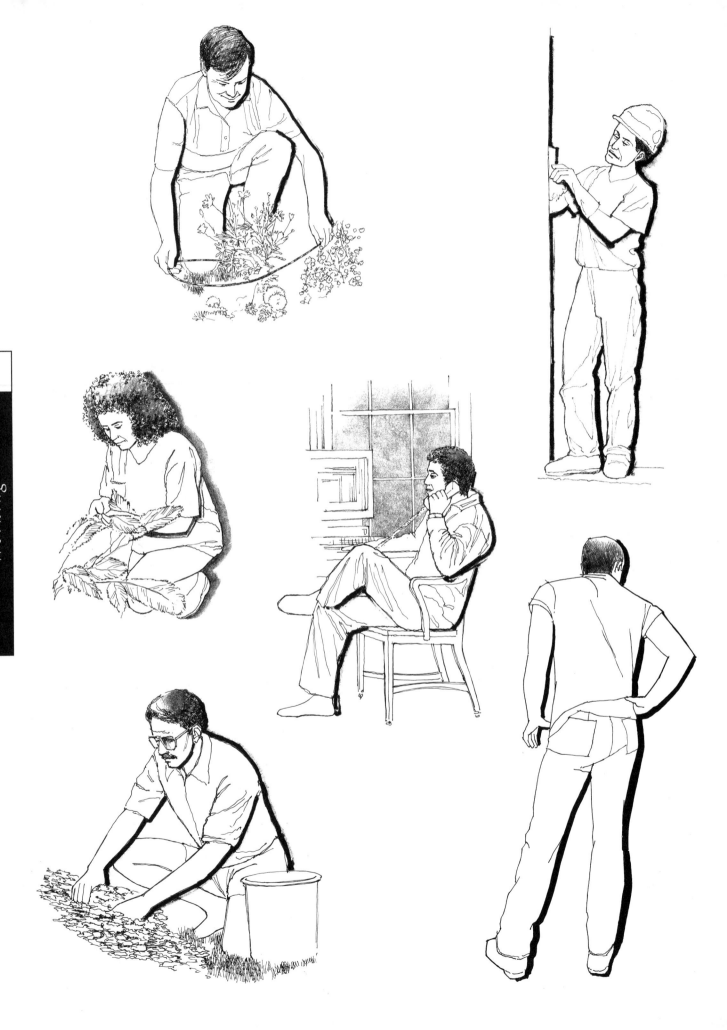

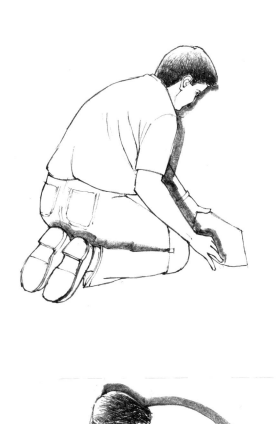

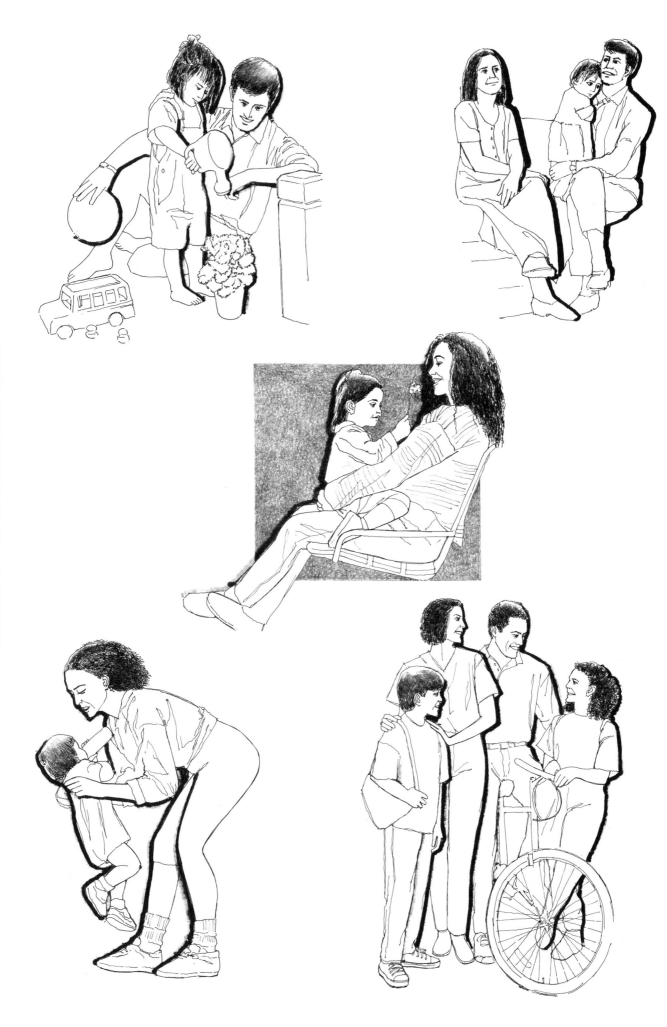

Parents with Kids

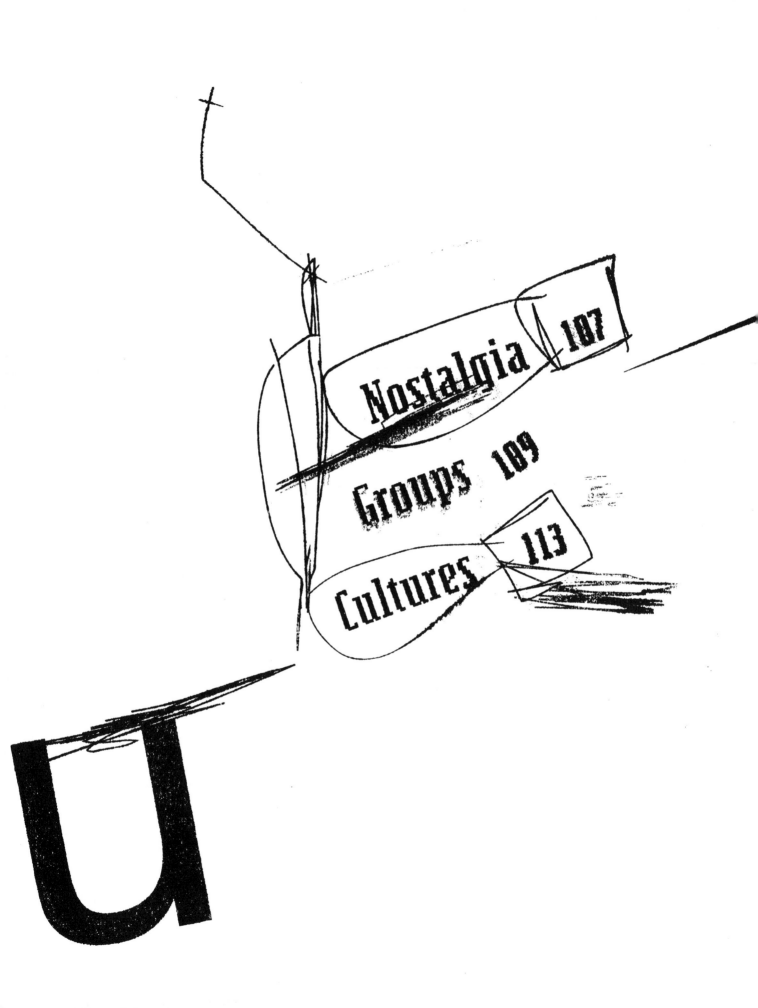

chapter four

e

peOple III

4

four

PEOPLE III

It was decided to group the categories of this chapter together because they would not be suitable for any other chapter.

Charm and warmth were meant to radiate from viewing the first category of Nostalgia. It simply could not be excluded from the book. I believe there will be use for it. The second category of Groups was essential to include the clustering and the resulting scale and depth when groups are represented in a project.

The third category of Cultures was a pivotal one. However, it was by no means possible to represent every culture.

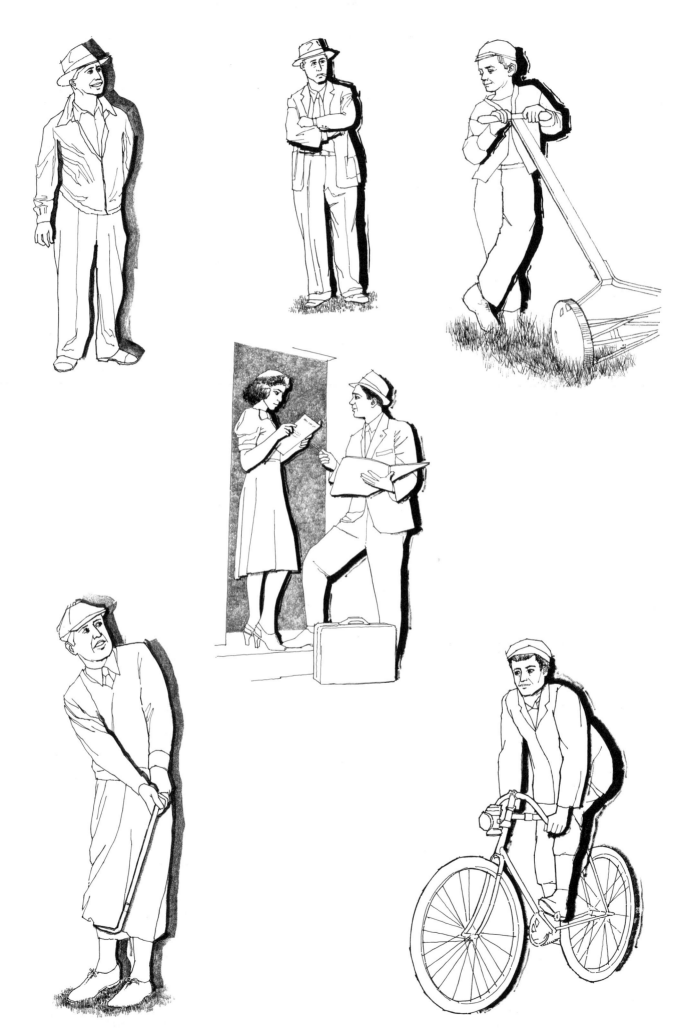

Cultures

CHAPTER 5IVE

people IV

MUSEUMS/GALLERIES
AND ELEVATIONS

In keeping with the objective of this publication, another worthy subject is represented in this chapter: viewing art in galleries and museums or similar spaces such as antique stores and auction houses needed to be included. It is not believed to be included anywhere in other publications of similar use.

Clearly for the purpose of convenience, people posing in orthographic posture on a flat ground line are portrayed in different scale ready to be traced for inclusion in elevational presentations.

Scaled Elevations

scale: 1/2" = 1'-0

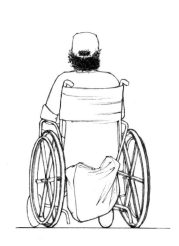

Scaled Elevations

scale: 1/2" = 1'-0

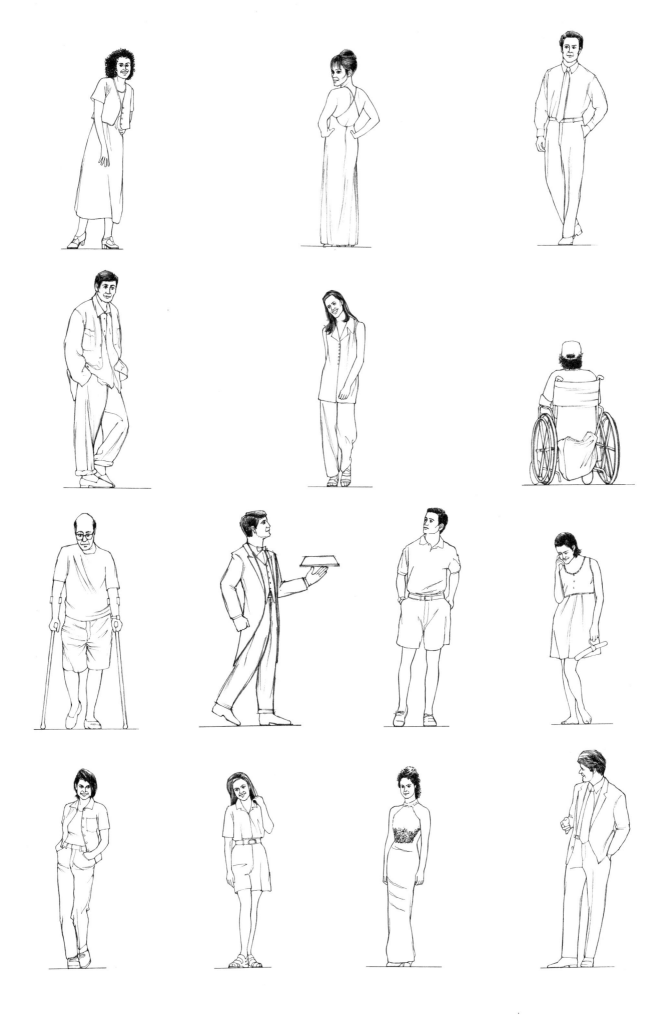

Scaled Elevations

scale: 3/8" = 1'-0

Scaled Elevations

scale: 1/4" = 1'-0

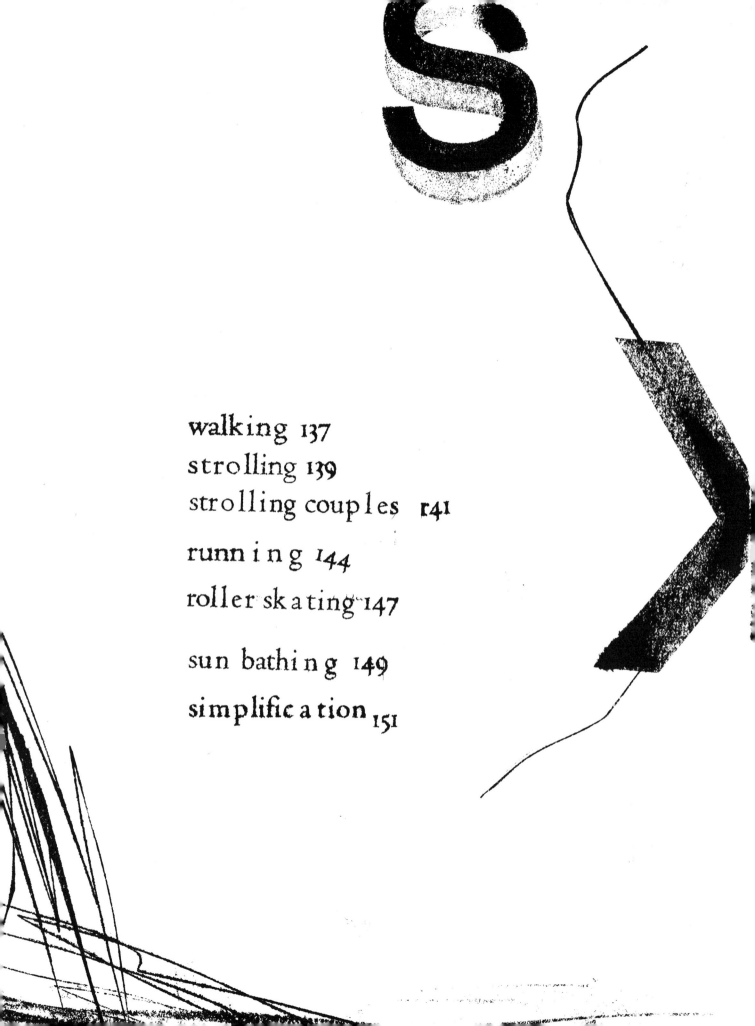

Chapter six

recreation I

6

RECREATION I

This chapter begins a series of three on recreation in different forms. This particular one addresses the simple ways to enjoy one's life as in walking, strolling, or running alone or with company. It also includes a pleasant and quite mobile recreational hobby in roller skating, an activity hardly ever represented.

Swimming suits are indicated to represent either poolside or beach recreation.

Strolling Couples

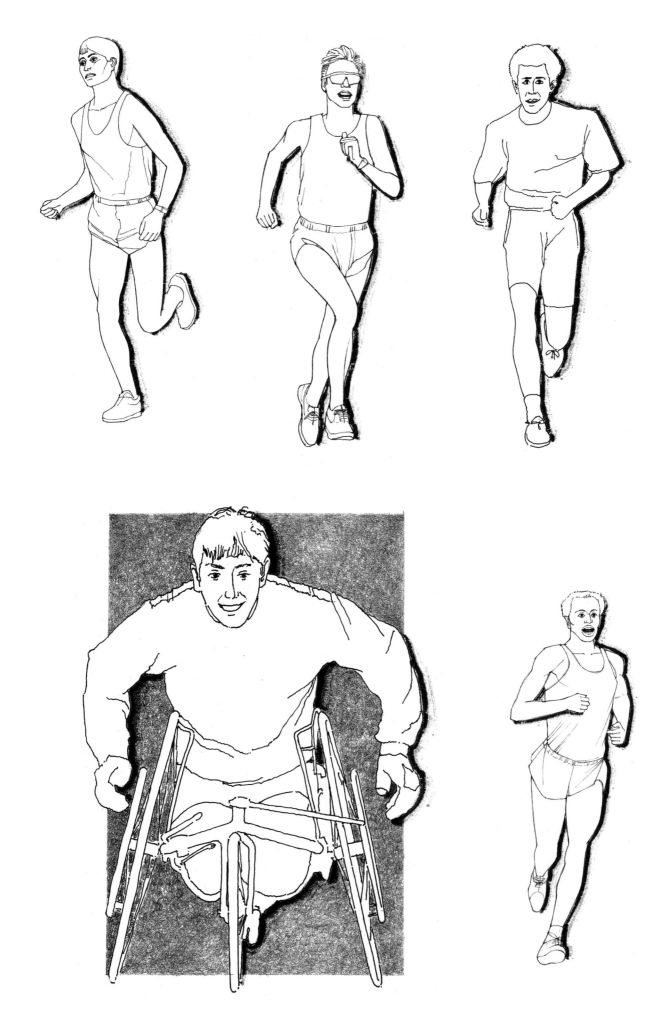

Roller skating

Sunbathing

chapterseven

recreation II

RECREATION II

In this chapter, I tried to get into a different area of recreation. It gets into more personal and sometimes private situations. This is especially indicated in the categories of Couples in Harmony and Relaxing Together. Other categories that I believe are pure expression and lively are Animated People and Goofing Off.

A category that can be quite useful in specific project presentations is the one on Dancing. This one includes a subcategory that is hardly ever represented in this form on traditional Belly Dancing.

The category on Relaxing was most interesting to me. In selecting images to interpret, I had to imagine myself in each posture and feel all my muscles relaxed.

Animated People

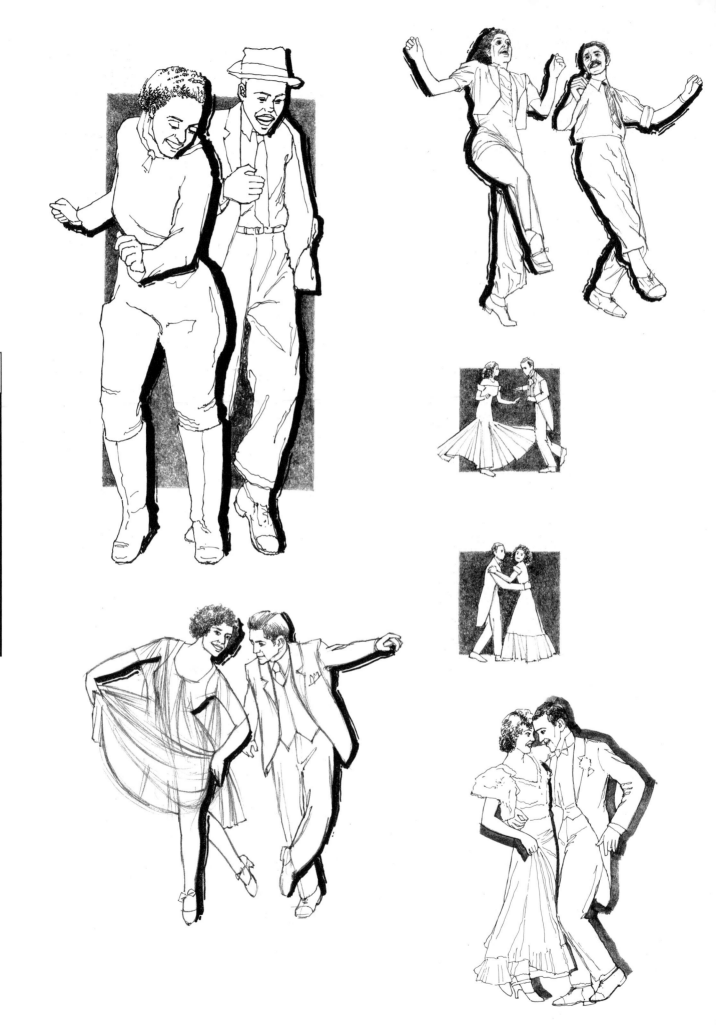

after Von Kaulbach

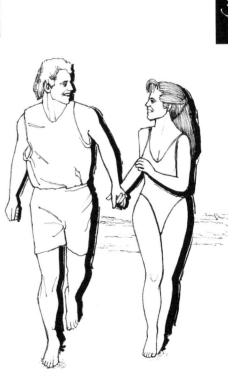

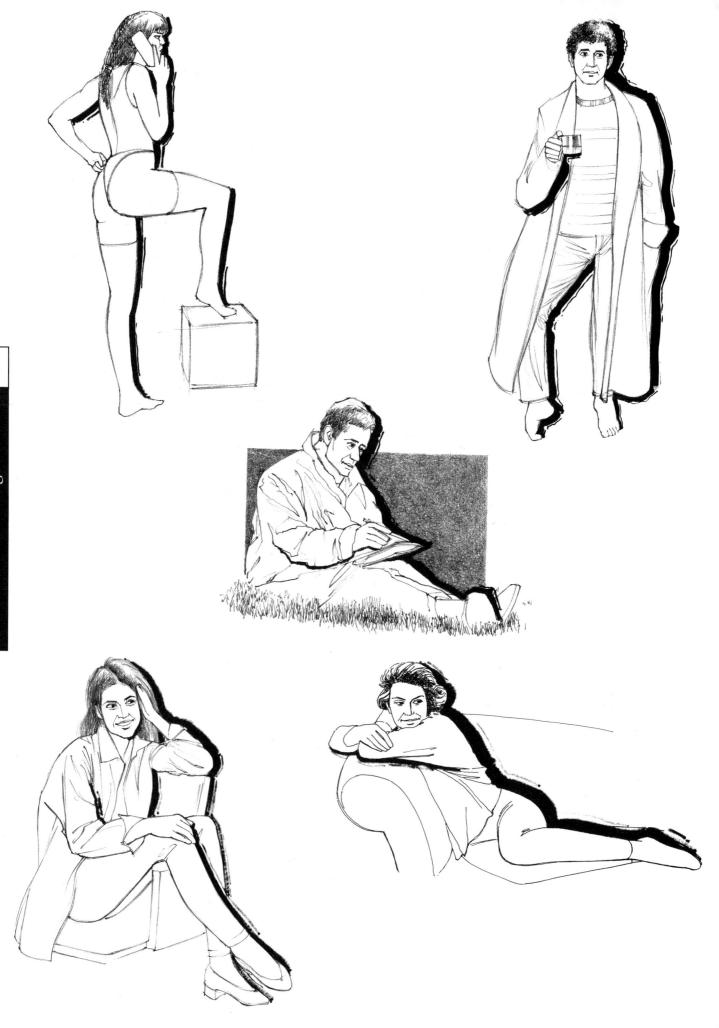

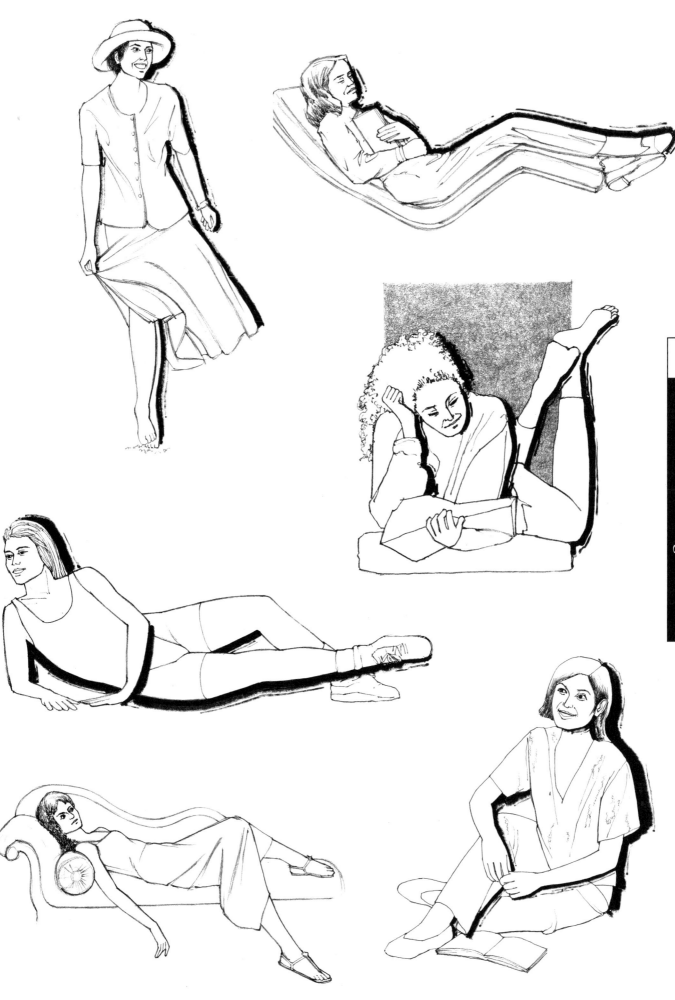

Relaxing

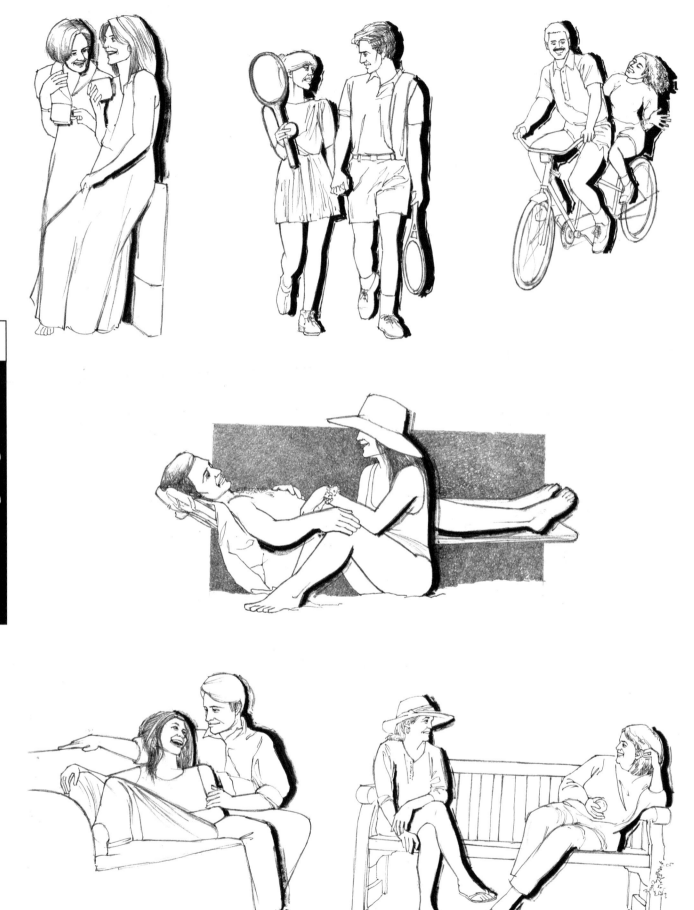

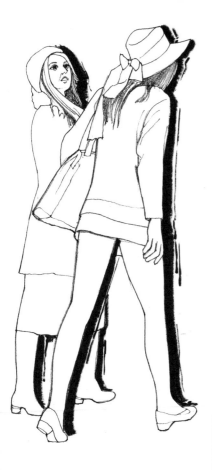

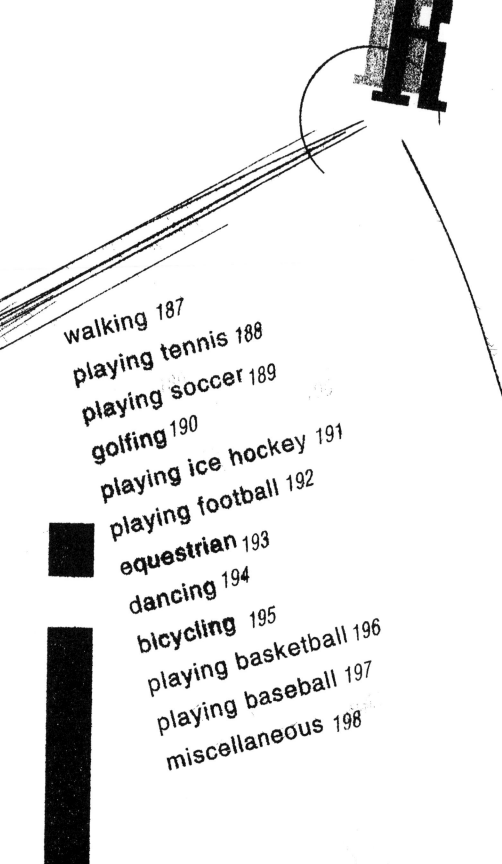

chapter eight

RECREATION III 8

RECREATION III

It was rather intimidating to think that one should include all known sports in this chapter. Obviously, that was impossible and unnecessary. A serious attempt, however, was made to include the sports most readily known to most of us. Selections of animated gestures were made to portray the major characteristics of each sport and communicate its essence to the reader for easy access and use.

In keeping with the intended comprehensive nature of this book, the sophisticated sport of Equestrian was included.

The miscellaneous section was added where there was not enough material for a sport, .

Walking

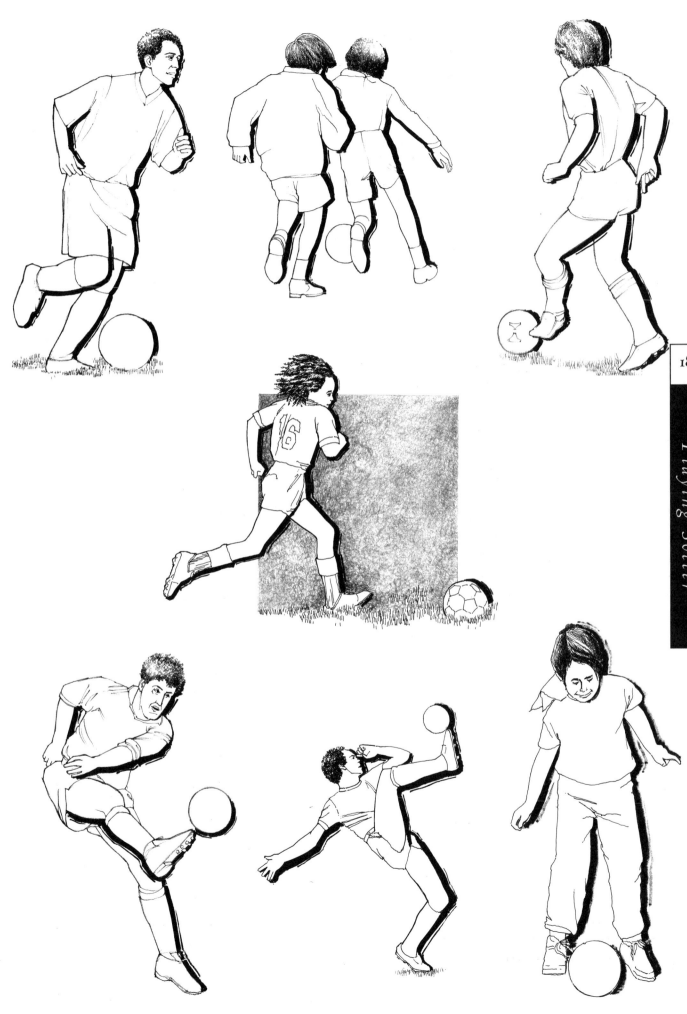

Playing Soccer

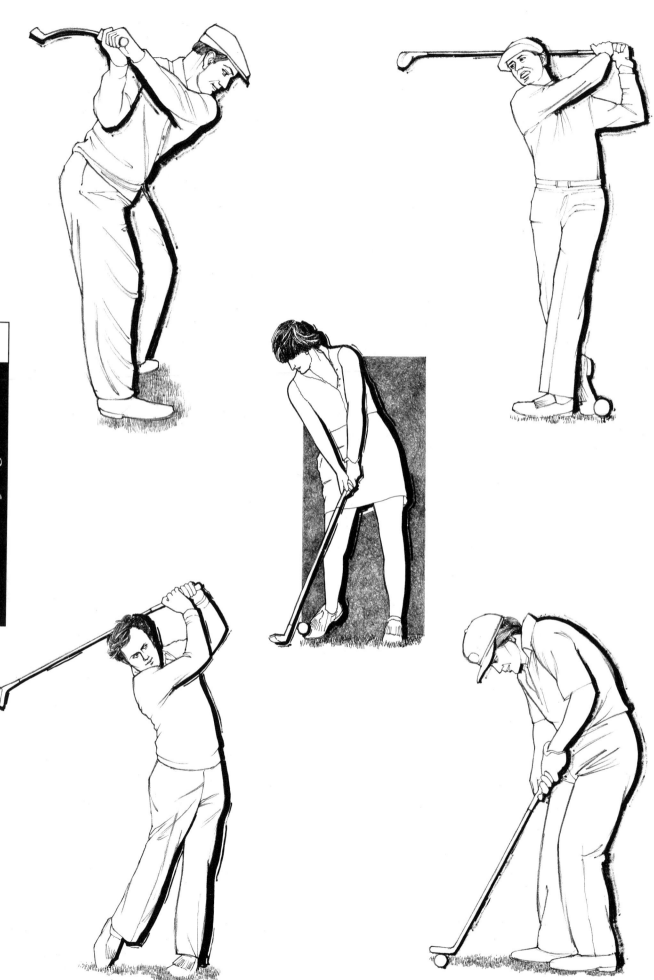

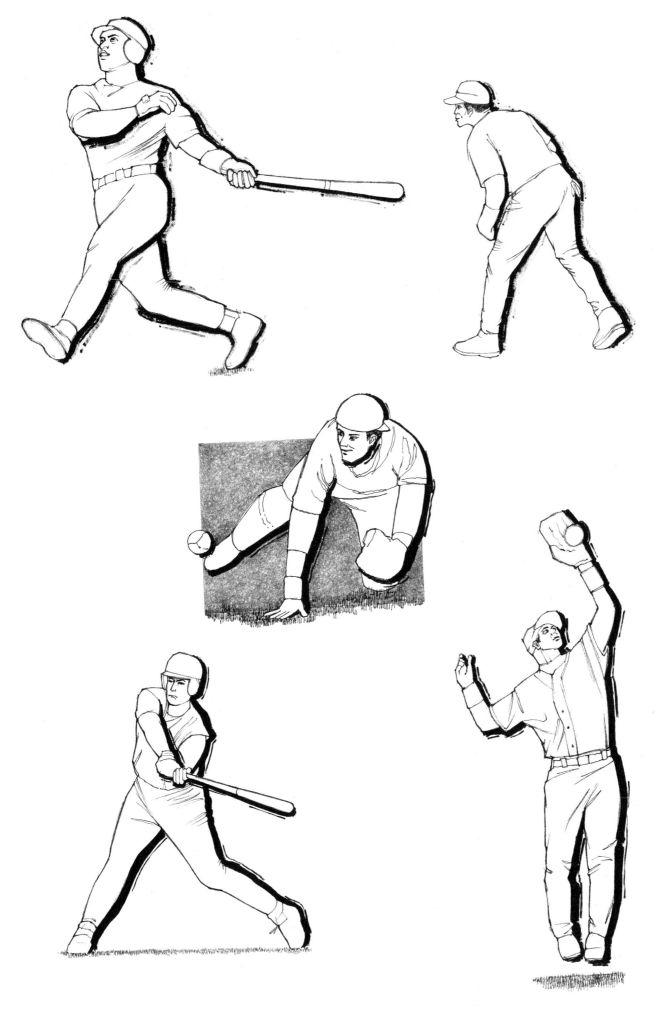

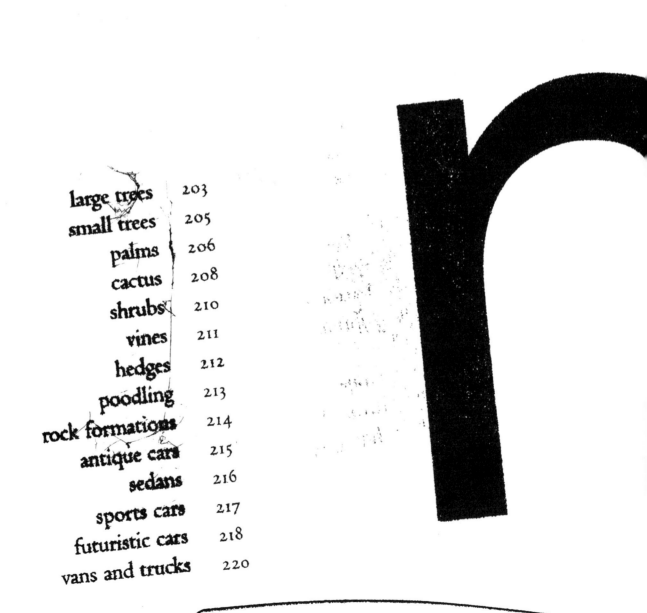

chapternine

exteriordesign

EXTERIOR DESIGN

The interdisciplinary spirit of learning and cooperation between many professions and the merging of gray areas between them prompted me to include the content of this chapter. Exterior Design presentations, whether architecture or landscape architecture, necessitate the inclusion of vegetation in various forms and scale. A comprehensive representation of landscape elements is indicated for a reasonable ease of selection by the reader/ user.

Moving vehicles are represented in several subcategories starting from the 1920's and projecting into the early 21st century, which includes a flying car.

Large Trees

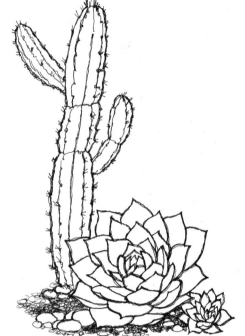

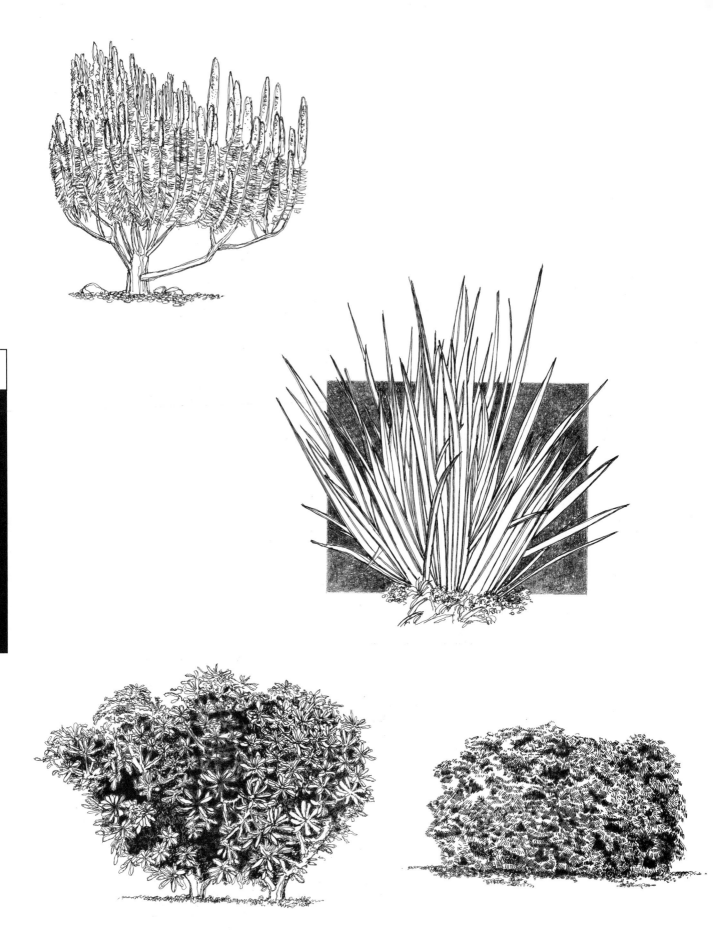

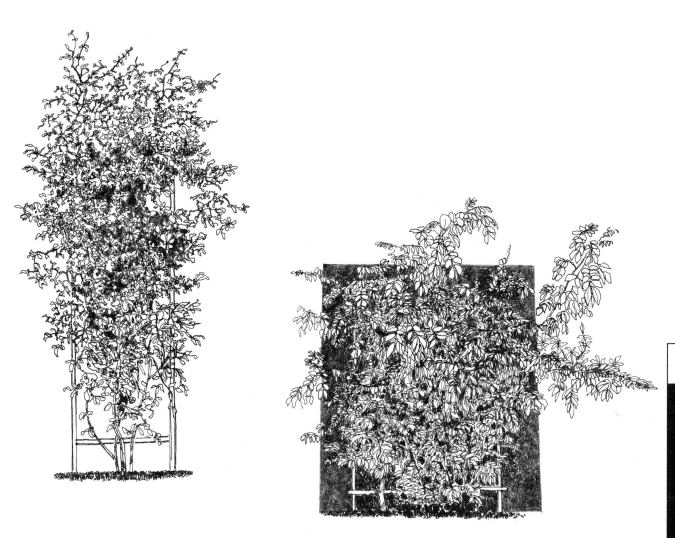

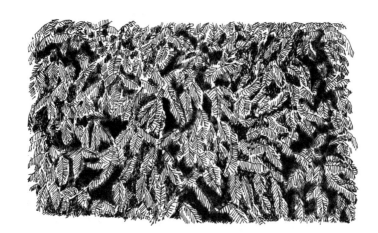

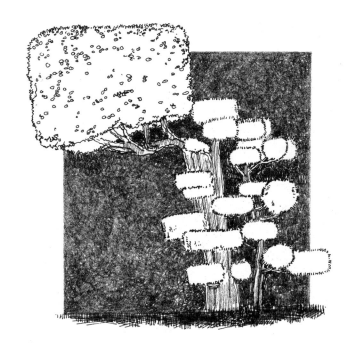

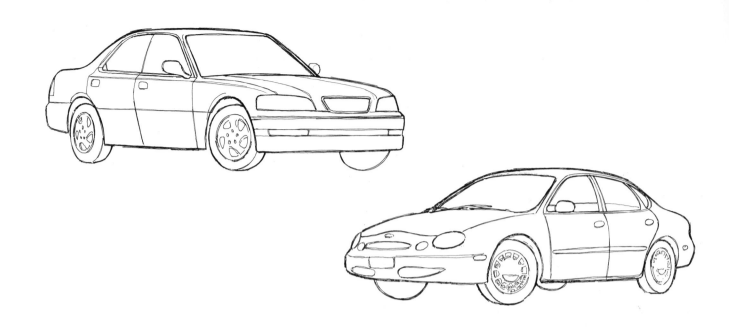

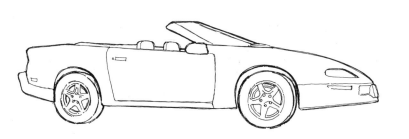

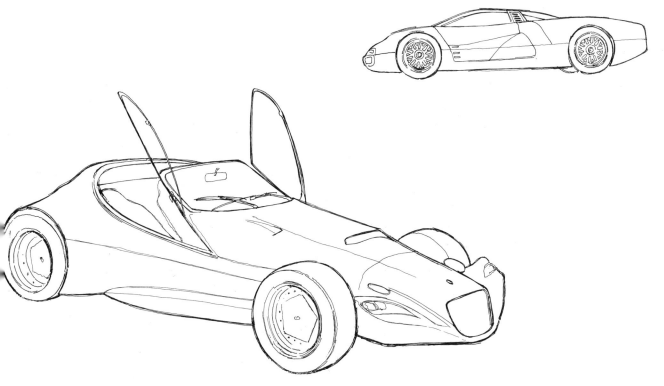

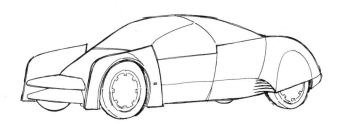

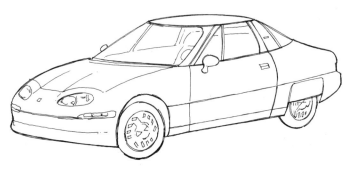

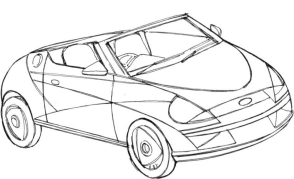

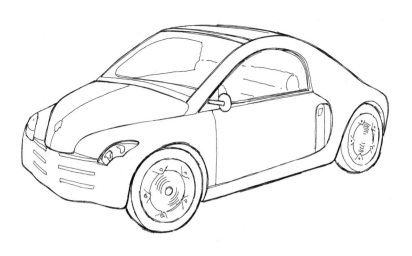

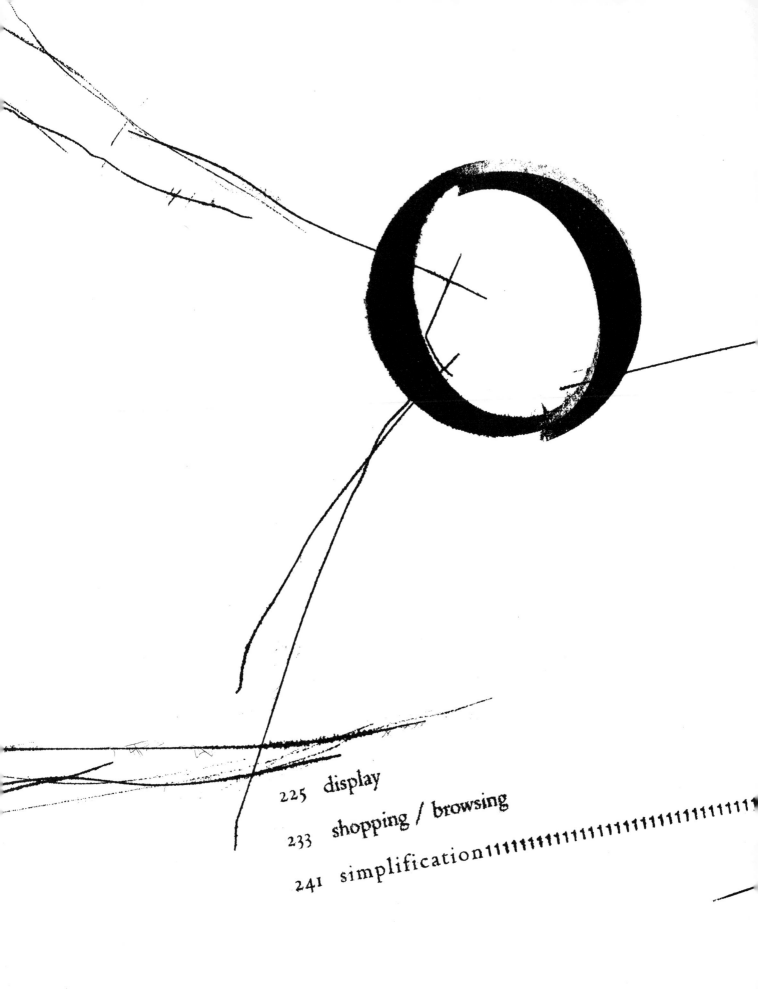

chapter ten

RETAIL DESIGN

10

RETAIL DESIGN

In this chapter, two major categories pertain to different sides of the subject. It is viewing or being viewed. It's either browsing/shopping or displaying.

As merchandising increases in prominence in the retail design vocabulary, variety and innovation in display techniques and mannequin postures are greatly needed. While natural postures are predominant in the display group of drawings, they sometimes may need to be used as the basis for different styles to suit the project at hand.

Shoppers have a variety of attitudes. There are those who browse curiously, surveying the available merchandise, with no intent of purchase. There are also those who are looking and thinking indecisively and have the time to do it. Meanwhile, there are those who are on the run. If there is a need for portraying shoppers with kids, drawings can be found in Chapter Three under the subchapter Parents with Kids.

Display

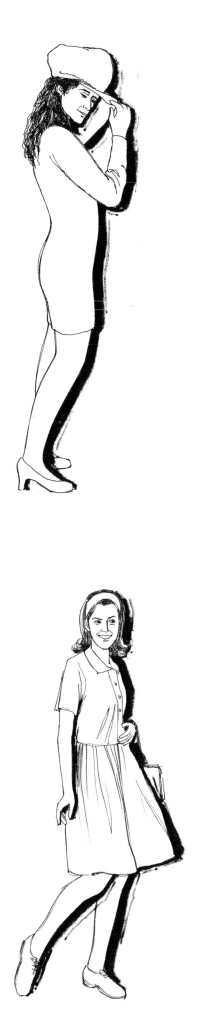

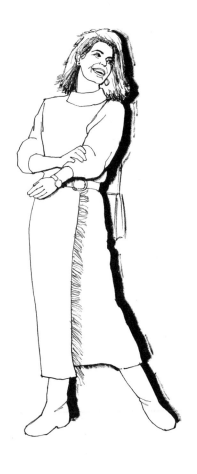

Simplification

CHAPTER ELEVEN

office design

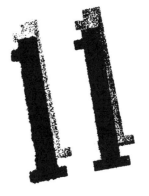

11

OFFICE DESIGN

Categories in this chapter are as direct as the subject requires. The one category that was most important was Impromptu Meetings. It is one that is a most frequent occurrence in a company setting.

The Group Meetings category can be used for many variations and partial utilizations.

The Workers category represents a wide variety of individual activities, from CEO to secretary. It includes a host of situations from reception counter, to computer worker, to phone conversations, to workers on breaks, etc.

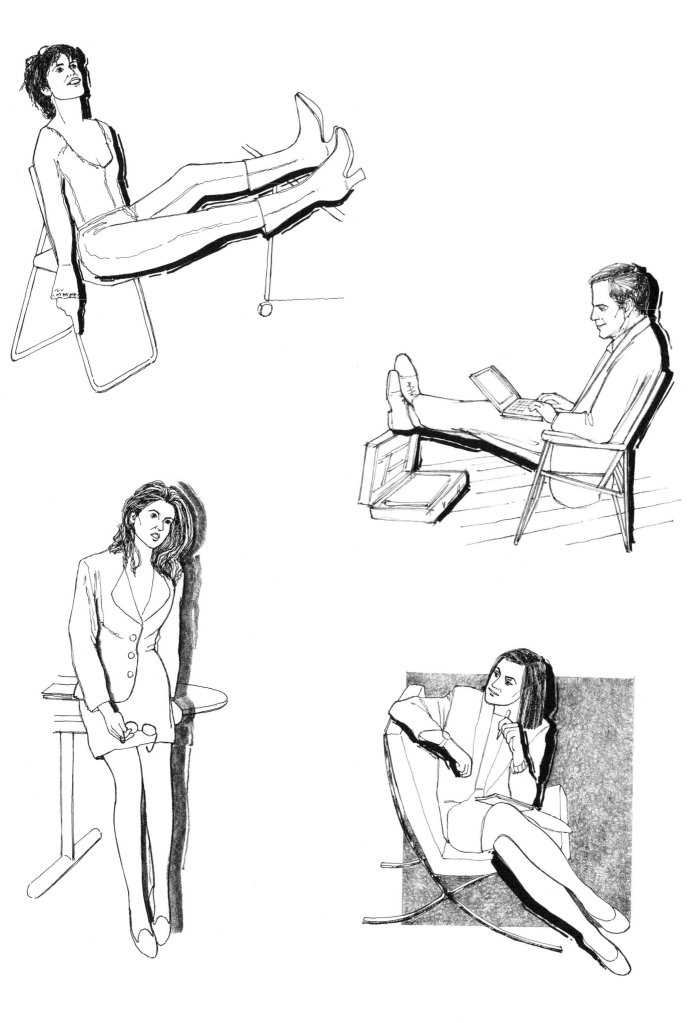

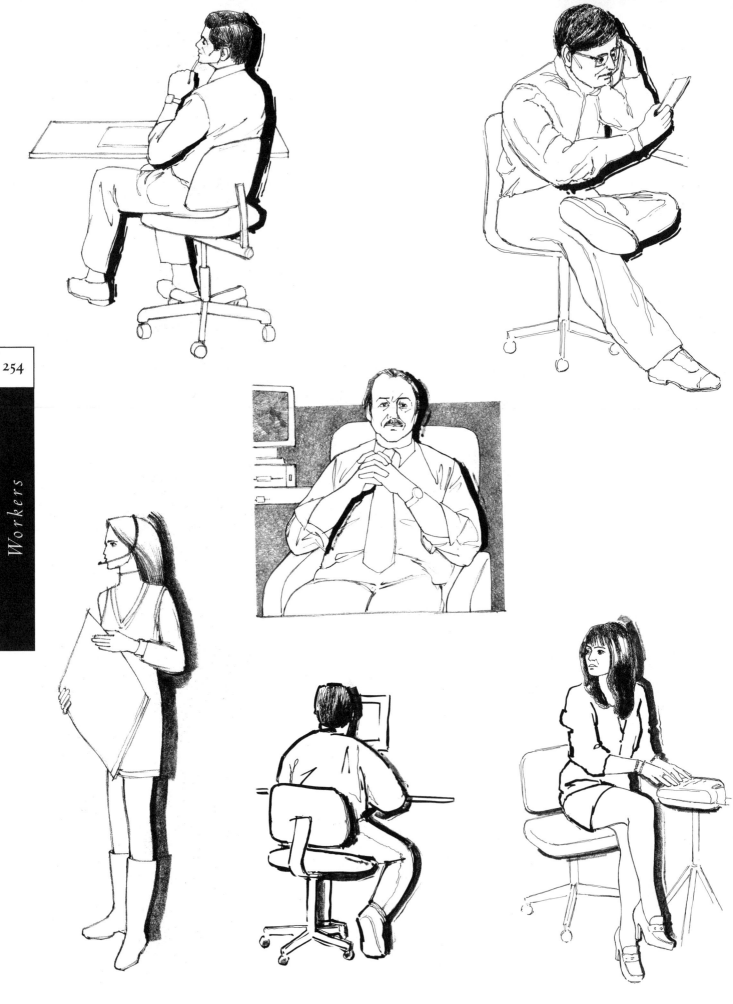

CHAPTER TWELVE

healthcare design

12

HEALTHCARE DESIGN

Due to the aging of the U.S. population, healthcare issues are taking prominence in the national debate. The healthcare design field and industry are also moving to meet the challenge.

Paramount in this chapter is responding to the A.D.A. (Americans with Disabilities Act) and the Barrier Free codes. This means accessibility made equally to healthy and wheelchair-bound people as well as the blind and all handicapped citizens in public spaces. Representations of doctors include visiting their patients in hospital rooms, working with nurses, and their action in surgery rooms. Nurses were indicated especially as they help patients.

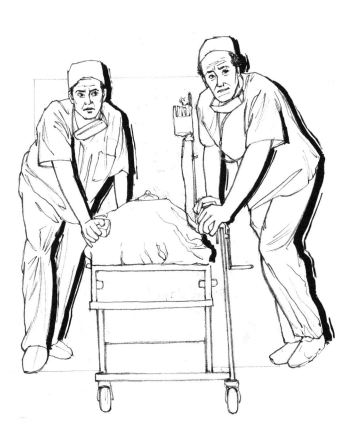

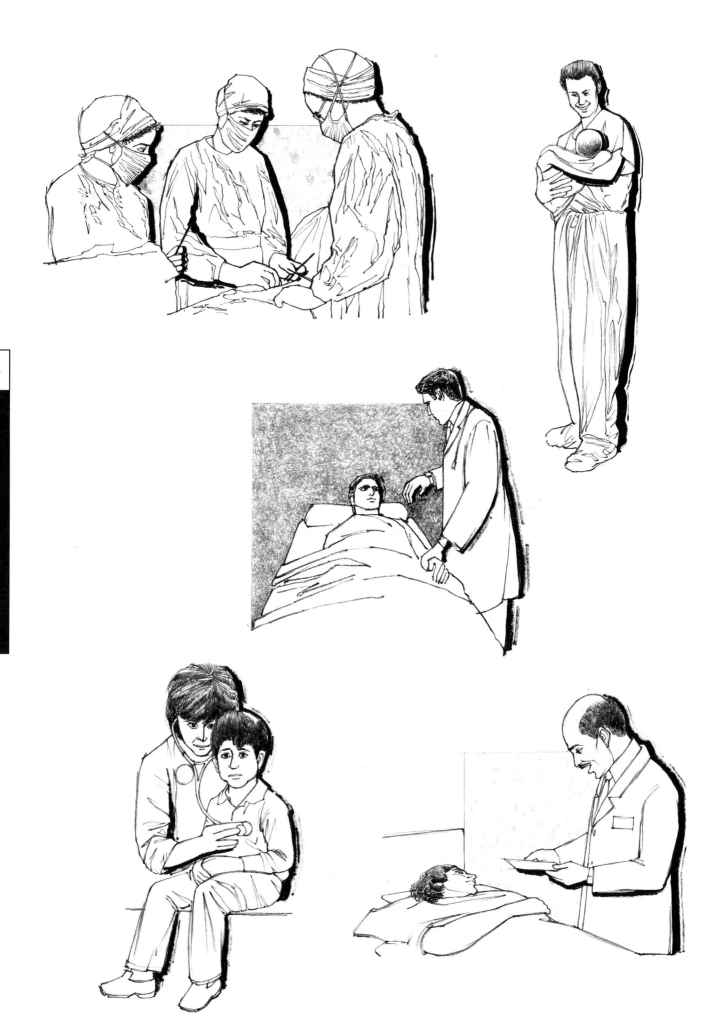

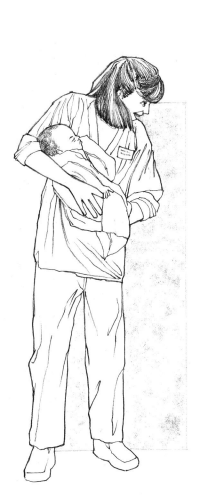

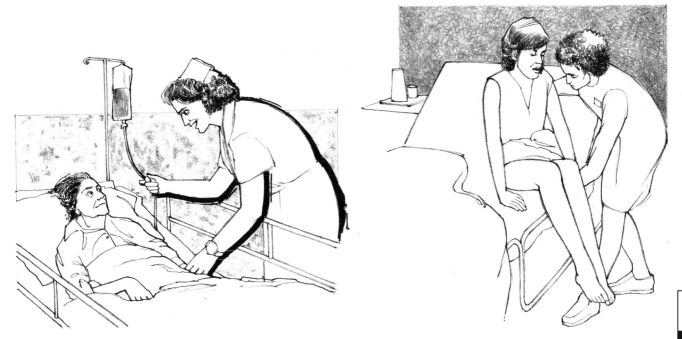

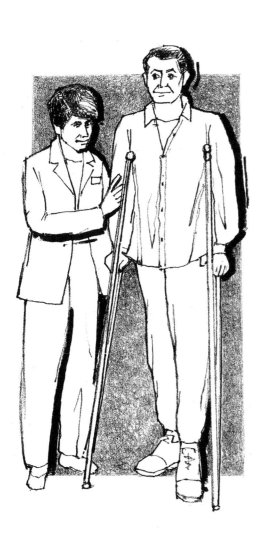

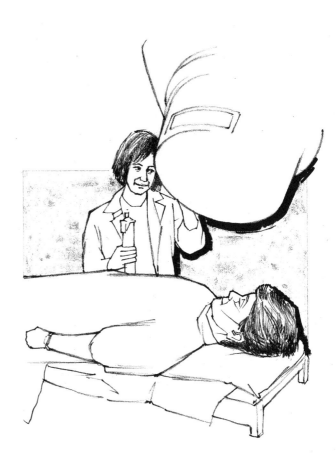

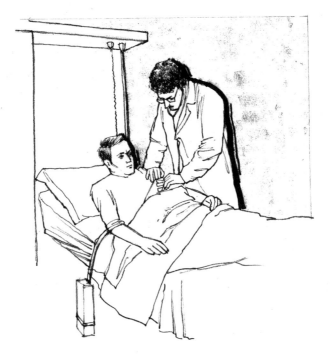

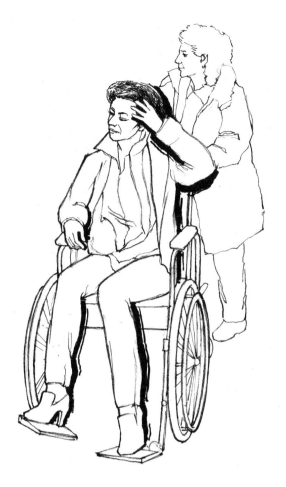

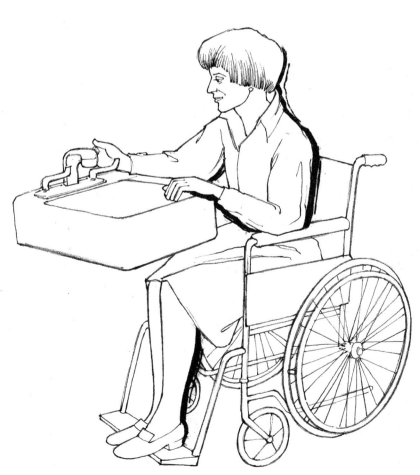

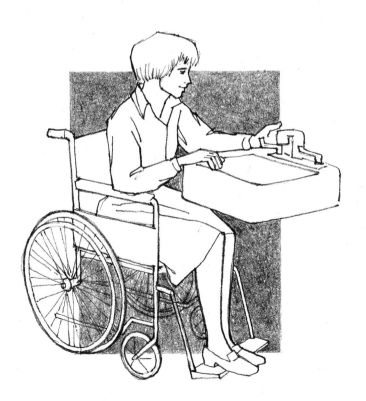

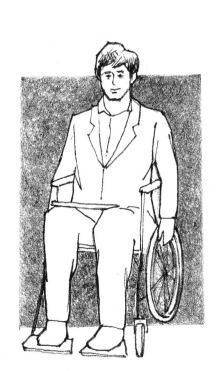

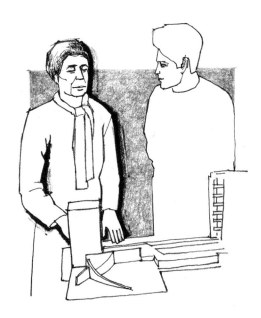

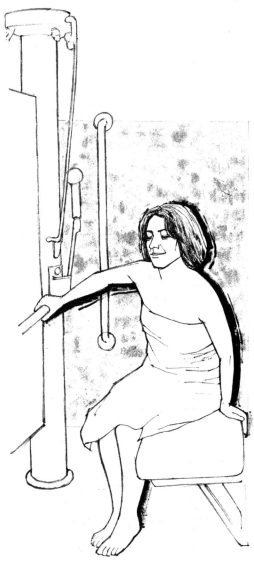

h

i

chapter
thirteen

HOSPITALITY DESIGN 13

HOSPITALITY DESIGN

This chapter addresses a wide range of hospitality design, starting from the coffee shop to the sidewalk or terrace cafe. Both of these categories are characterized by newspaper reading and chats.

In a restaurant setting, more time is spent. In these categories, customers have different attitudes about time and space. In the category of bars, there is a relaxed atmosphere with a lot of smiles and sparkling glances.

In hotel lobbies, there are people doing business and waiting, coming in or leaving. In hotel rooms guests are planning their trips or getting ready for the night out.

Cafes

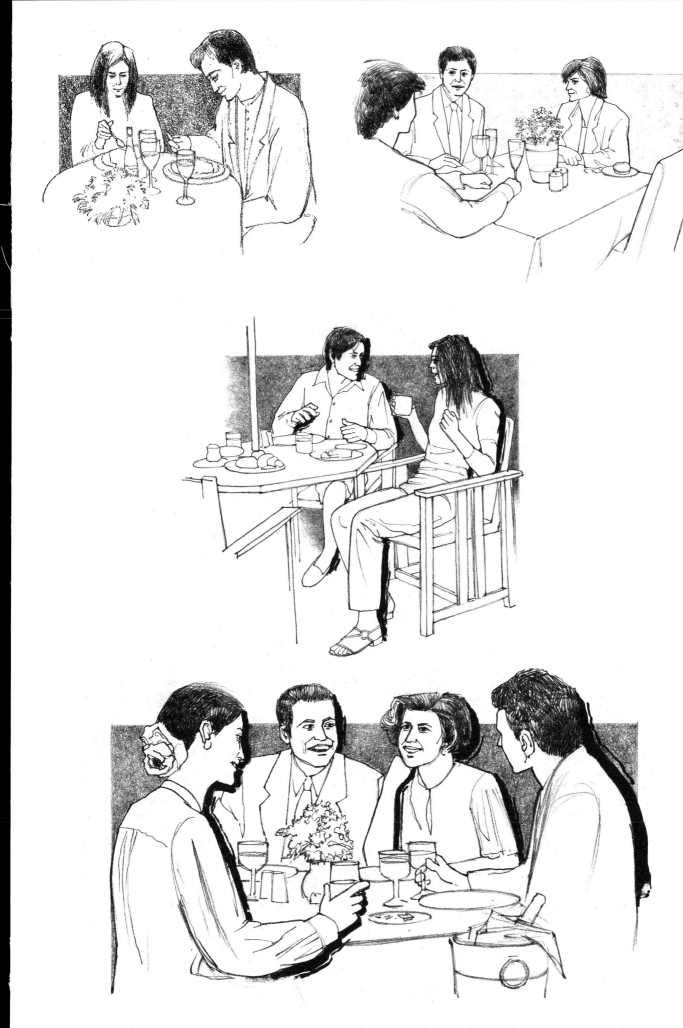

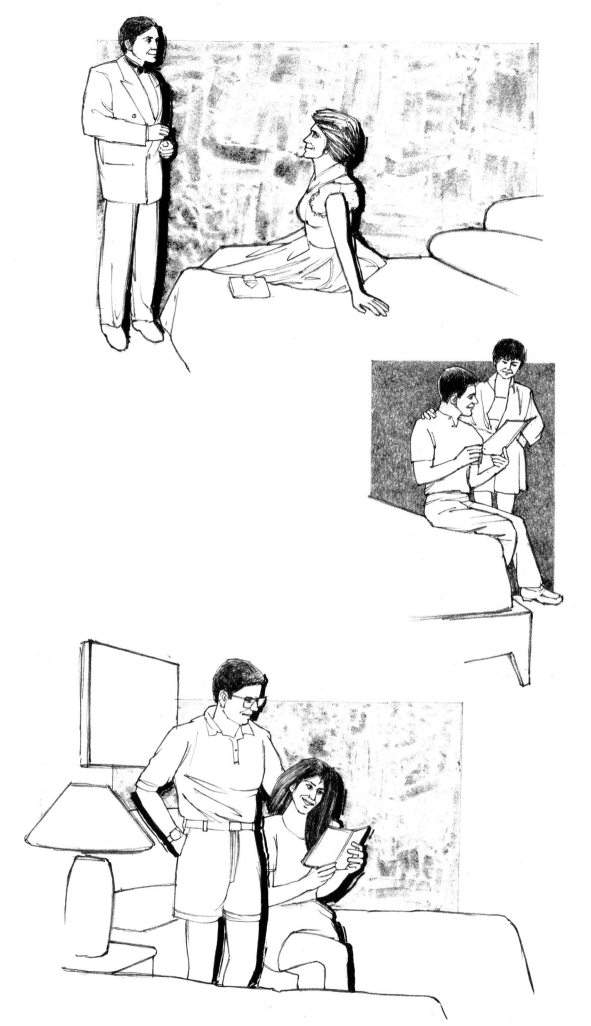

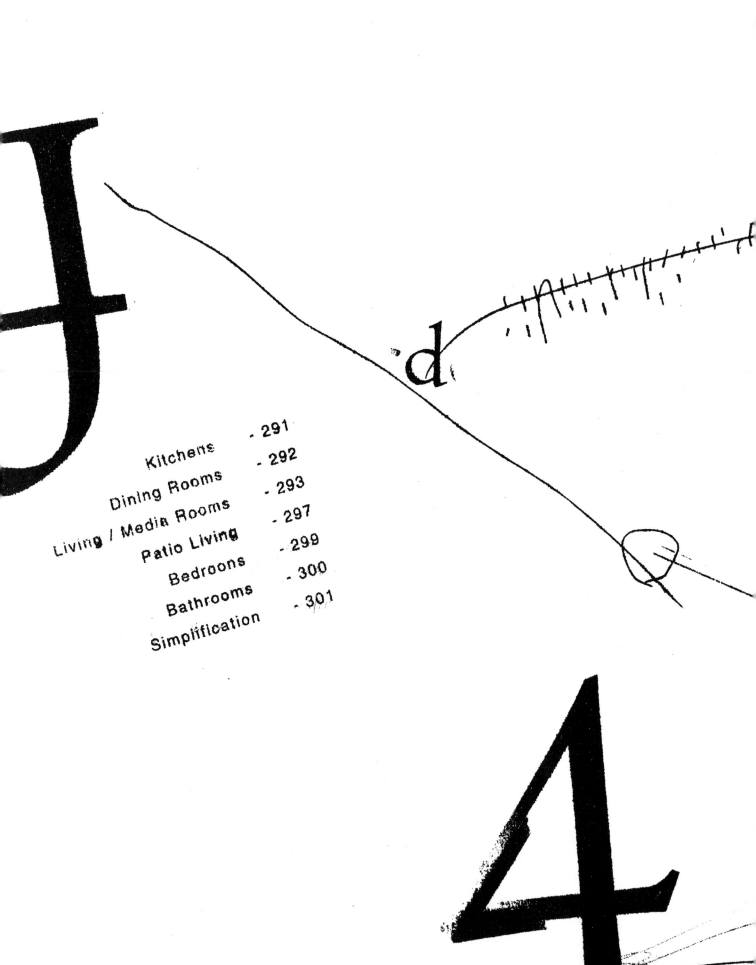

4

residential design

14

RESIDENTIAL DESIGN

The field of residential design is a very wide one. My approach to this was to emphasize the main parts of a residence, starting with the kitchen and moving on to dining rooms to living or media rooms.

Bedrooms and bathrooms are hardly ever addressed in this form in any publication.

The category that I believe was quite interesting to address was patio living. Preparing food and enjoying terrace or poolside get-togethers can be indicated to enhance exterior design project presentations.

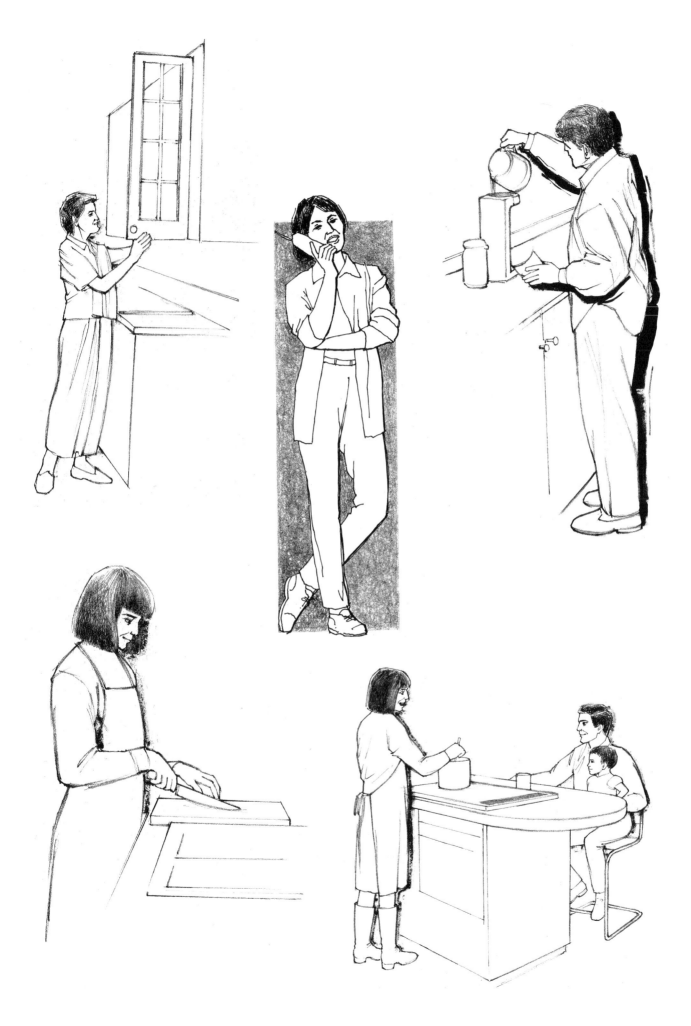

Dining Rooms

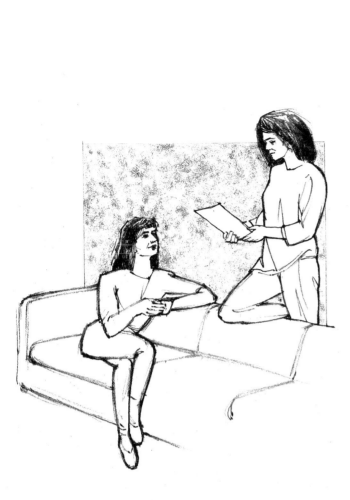

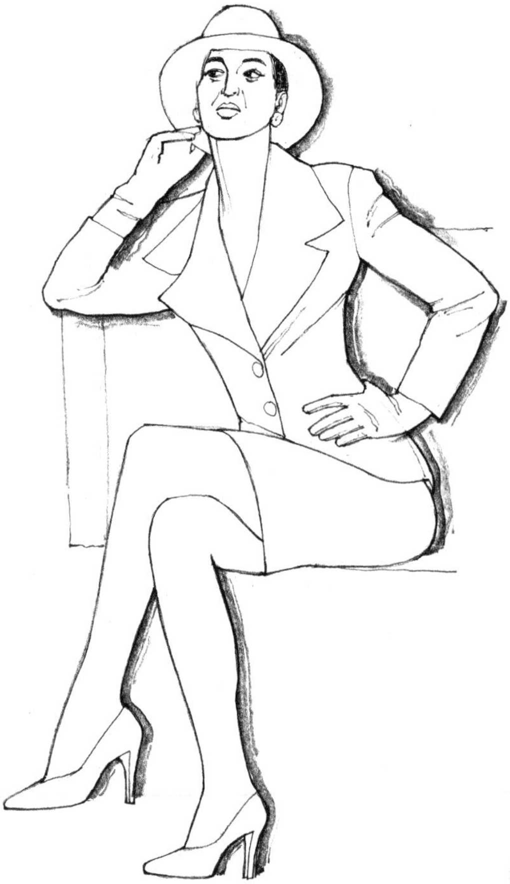

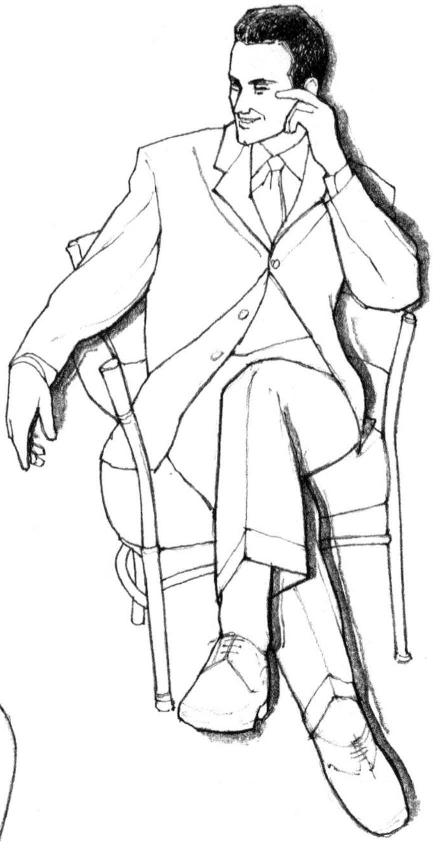

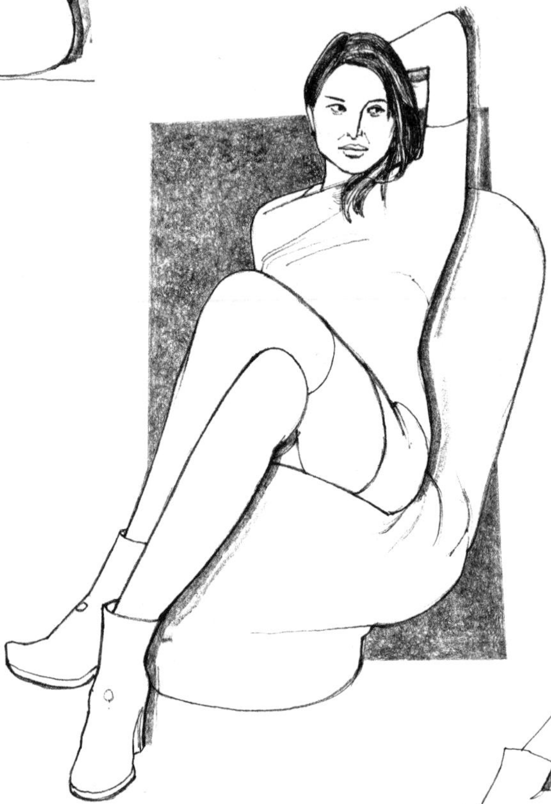

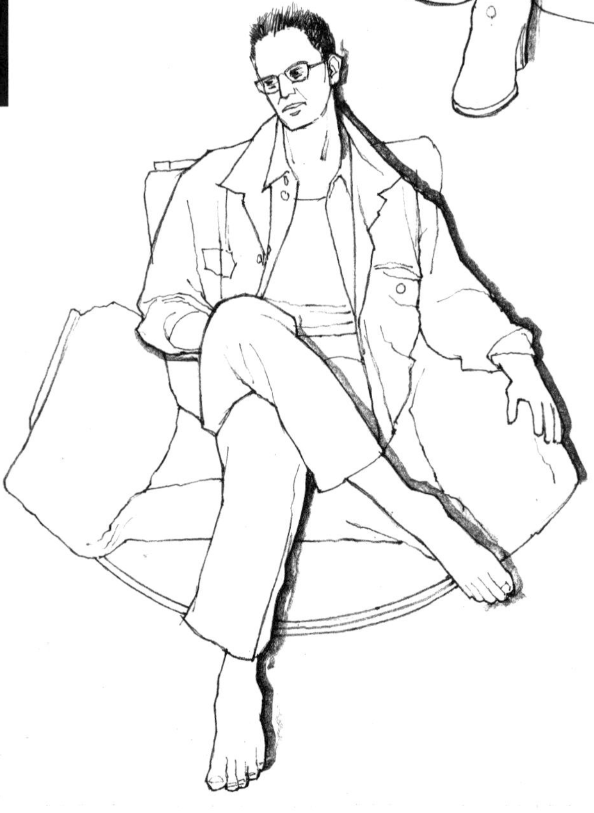

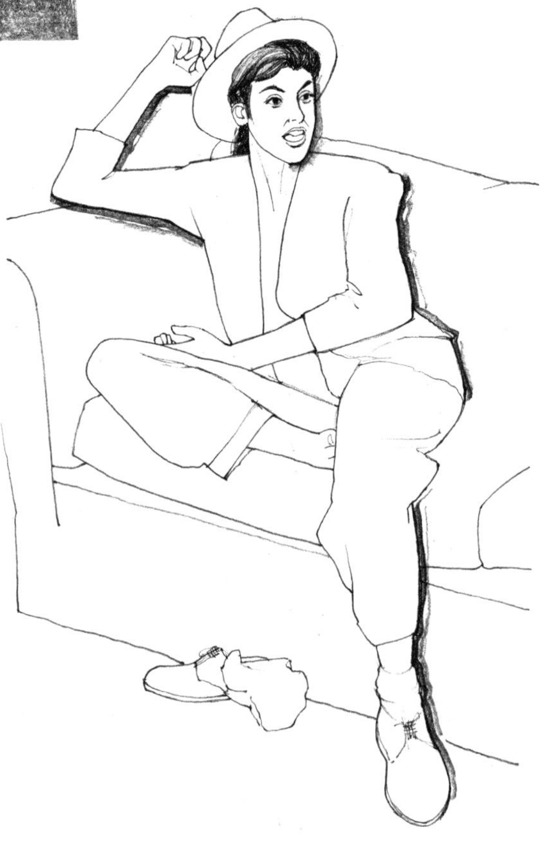

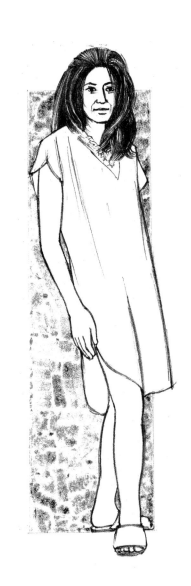

Bathrooms

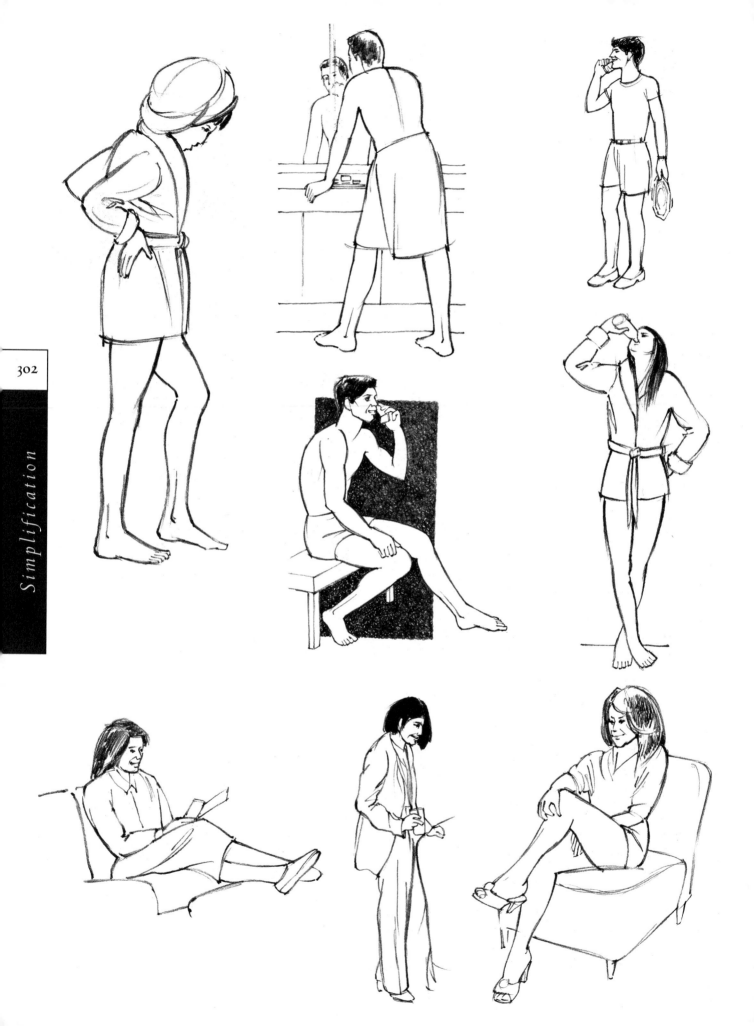

15

(chapter fifteen)

stuvwxyz

accessories

15

ACCESSORIES

The lack of resources in this particular area in any publication was identified by several of my colleagues and students. This prompted this chapter, which will hopefully facilitate the inclusion of rich accessories in project presentations.

The collection of accessories is particularly important. Relating accessorizing to aesthetics only in interior design can be sometimes perceived as indulgent. I encourage the use of objets d'art as a vehicle to pointing out art history and cultural diversity. Elements such as bonsai and floral arrangements are largely neglected in many project presentations whether by students or professional interior designers.

Both planting materials and objets d'art should fit the setting. Both the student and the professional are encouraged to go beyond familiar species towards the more unusual and culturally appropriate.

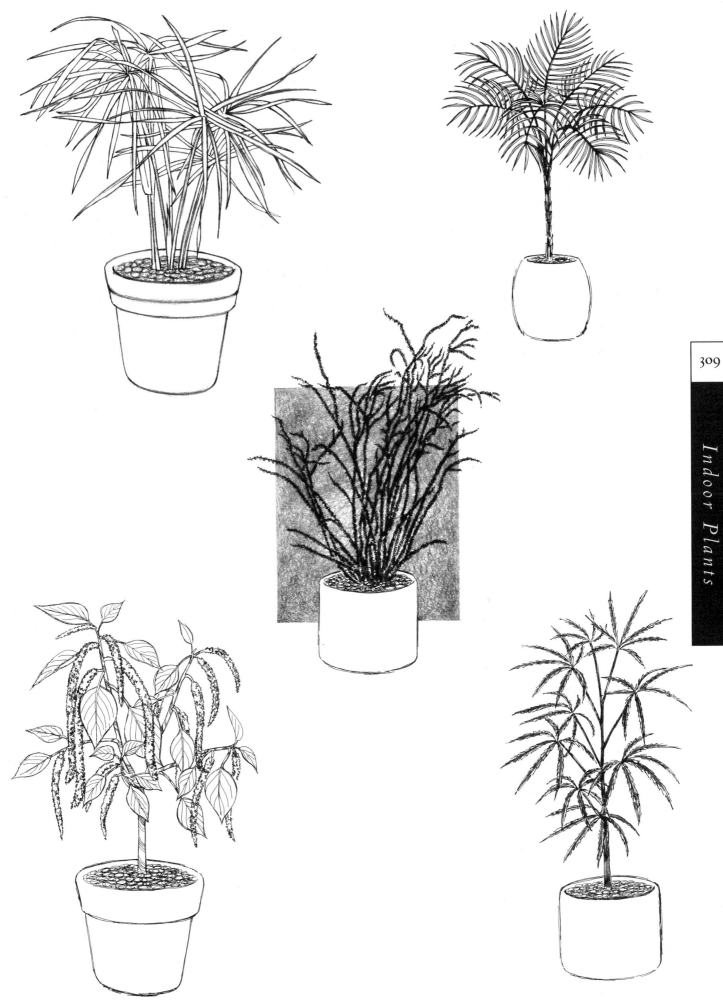

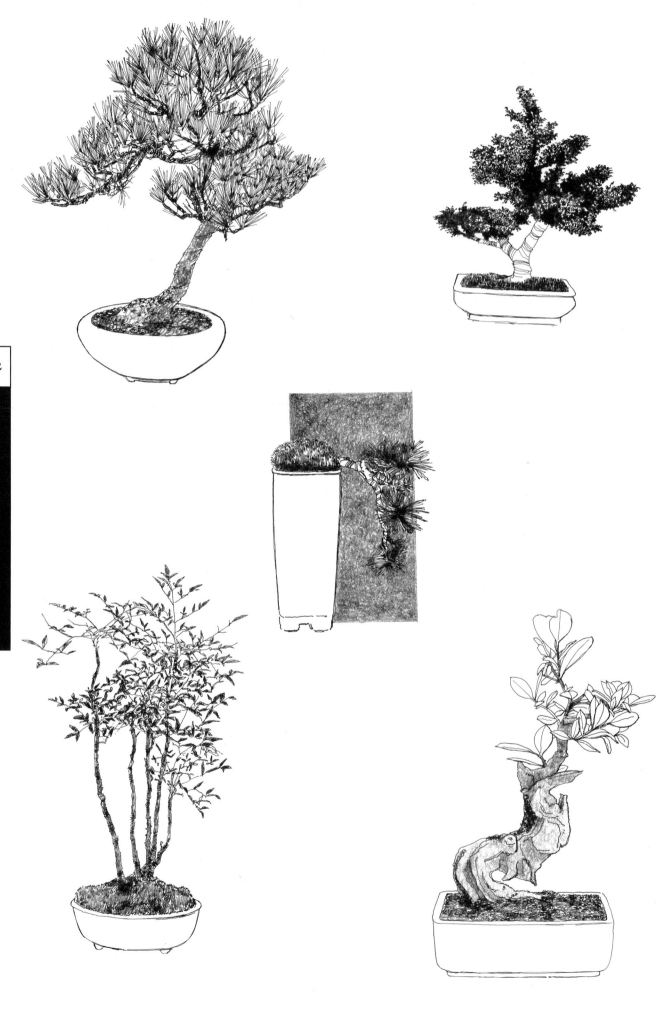

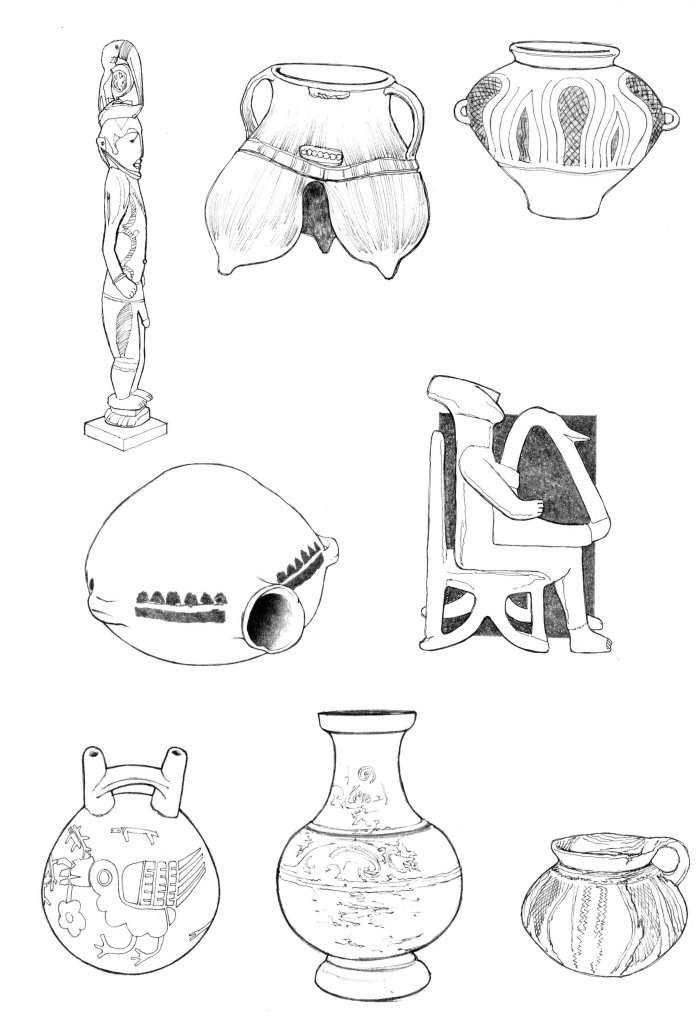

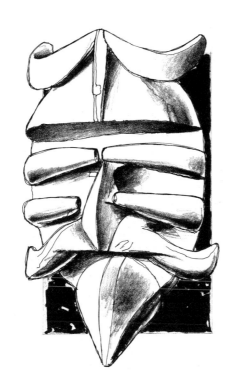

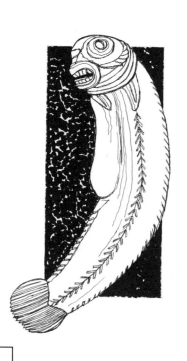

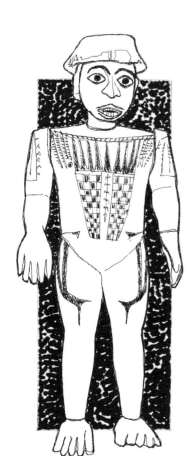

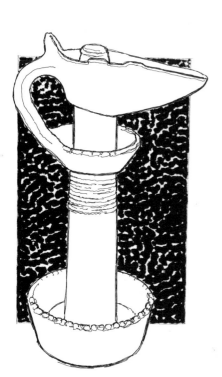

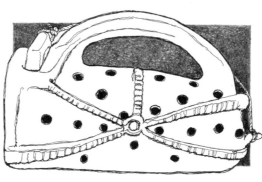

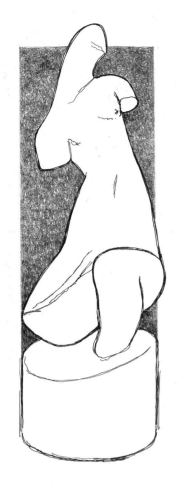

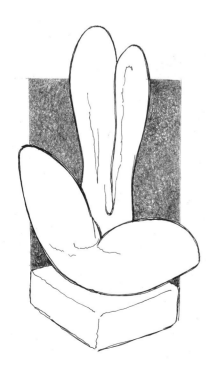

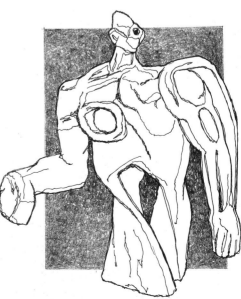

Modern Abstract